Mischa Hammarnejd

Song of Being

– the end of searching –

Song of Being

© Mischa Hammarnejd, 2023

Headlines: Didot
Body text: Baskerville
Descriptive text: Futura

Publisher: BoD – Books on Demand, Stockholm, Sweden

Print: BoD – Books on Demand, Norderstedt, Germany

ISBN: 978-91-8027-938-3

Content

A short summary about Mischa can go here...

An unusually curious and truth-hungry boy grew up relatively unhindered and free, got wings in the new world of computers, made strong efforts to explore the inner essence of Christianity (which he did not see truth* and depth in until recently!), surfed happily* – enthusiastically applauded – on the new wave of digitizing the pre-press and printing industry, held fast to the path of knowledge that was so open, sought after, and enticing, and he came to what he believed was the beginning of a life of utmost satisfaction. But, alas, how he deceived himself! His life was – albeit lined with deep reflection and some arduous perseverance – built on the quagmire of change and subjectivity, like the house built on sand. Almost without warning, he was suddenly alone – but the journey that this book tells the story of, had already begun, and he had a feeling that something very vast and mystical* would be revealed before his eyes. That is what happened.

During ten solar revolutions, he has now bathed in understandings and experiences* that there is very little room for in the western and materialistically* dualistic* culture that he was brought up in. One of the completely unexpected fruits of these solar revolutions, is this little book. But he continues to enjoy the intimacy of Being and explores its infinite forms and expressions, without ambition or searching. Where the path leads to and what may come does not trouble him any longer, for now it has become true: Home is where the heart is, and he has never left it.

Disclaimer

As my native language is Swedish and not English, I ask the reader for tolerance and patience. Also, when writing from the experiences like I do, it often happens that it is very difficult or even impossible for me to use correct grammar, even in Swedish. The attentive reader will take note of this.

Preface

Mischa is a name given to a form, figure, person* who listens when that name is mentioned.

The person called Mischa is on one hand nothing special, is not special in any way. On the other hand, there is no other person like this one, so in that way, it is special, just like all other persons (recently eight billion) are special. That this person is special, is therefore not very special…

But… **That which experiences** what it is like to be this person called Mischa, through quite a few solar revolutions now, is more than and that which contains this person. It expresses itself through this person, among others, and right now it is expressing itself through what is written in this book. In this context, I want to mention a few things:

- This book makes no claims of "the Truth" that I would possess and transmit to the reader. But, that I express something with this text, and that this text is understood in the reader, are experiences that are true. When what is expressed is understood in the reader, we meet – something in me merges with something in the reader, and this "something" is the same, identical in the experience. When this experience happens, we know, see, and feel it – because it is experienced! Enough said. All else would be to complicate what is true, and be completely unnecessary, because we already see, feel, and know that it is true.
- There is no direct purpose with this book. I only feel that something wants to be expressed. What is expressed is ultimately – or rather intimately – about what it is like to be the person Mischa, above all generally, and to some degree specifically. I wish that the reader remembers this throughout the reading – what it is like to be, to exist.
- Often, the expressions may sound as though I am upset about something, but that is not the case. It may sound that way because, in my particular mind*, there is something old and conditioned, the viewing things as black and white, a bit categorically. It has been my person's way to relate to various questions in life, due to many different things – but I hope that this does not cloud the reader's view.

- I am not trying to write in a way that appeals to the intellect, rather on the contrary, in order to reach what is before or hither, "on this side" of the intellect of the reader – just as the experiences that are described take place before or hither, on this side of my own intellect. This is why the writing doesn't follow any predetermined framework or rules, neither academic nor literary. But the writing still happens in a kind of pulse or rhythm that may look poetic, although that has not been my intent. The writing is done in a way that corresponds to how it felt when writing it, often a bit like breathing, one line per breath. Perhaps it benefits the reading and understanding if the texts are read in a similar fashion.
- There is a fundamental principle behind every piece; that it truly comes from the direct experience of what the text is about. In practice, when I am experiencing something – often very strongly and several times – I want to "document" the experience in some way, and thus double-check myself, to see if the experience is so clear that I can give it expression, as a kind of validation of its – and my – authenticity.
- Okey, there is another principle: Experience is a test of reality, since it is true, real* (and I don't mean *perception** – see the glossary for how experience and perception are often confused!) The experience is true. What is impossible to experience is therefore untrue, false. For example, we cannot experience a two-dimensional round square, which therefore is both experientially and conceptually* untrue, false. If you are inclined to dig deeper into what is called *empiricism,* you can. But I leave the scientific aside, because we already know that we experience, and we don't need any science or knowledge to neither prove nor validate what we already know. It is precisely this knowing, this seeing – before and on this side of the intellect – that I want to give expression to in this book.
- At the same time, I want to somehow de-mystify spirituality. There are many ways to view and describe what some call spirituality, but I see no reason to subscribe to any of them. It is possible for every human being to see, know, and feel what he really is, innermost, before all labels and titles are applied to the experience. It is from this place that these texts are born.
- If I quote somebody else's text, the source is given. Texts without a source are my own.
- In the glossary in the back of the book, there are words that, when used for the first time, are marked with an asterisk.

The structure of this book

While collating the texts for this book, texts written "along the way" on my journey, I notice a sort of structure. This structure becomes the chapters where the texts can land. The experiences that occur before and "on this side"of all texts, can be divided into different "themes," and the texts are sorted this way. Each chapter or theme is roughly in chronological order. For example, the exploration of the masculine & feminine happened fairly late on my journey. Within each chapter, the texts are also roughly in chronological order. This order is not important, they are still what they are and can stand on their own, or in a context.

I suspect that it seems so difficult for me to express in language, the understanding of this non-dual* reality, because language has been shaped for so long in a culture where this understanding was rare.

What is this book about?

I paint the seeing.
I paint with words.
Don't see my words.
Be the seeing.
The seeing on this side of the paper.
This side of our eyeballs that focus on the text.
This side of the understanding of the words.
This side of, this side of, this side of…
where there is only experience,
the experience of what the words point to.

As little as the artist who paints a painting
intends for the observer to see the paint
and how the brushstrokes are made,
do I intend for you to see my words.

The artist intends for the observer to see the motif
in the same way that the he saw it
when he painted it.
The artist intends for the observer to see
in the same way that the artist saw,
and therefore to be the artist's seeing.

In the same way, I intend for you
to see what the words point to,
namely the experience of being
that which experiences,
that you can see what my words describe,
and therefore be the same seeing that I am.

When you read these words
about what it is that experiences,
you most likely feel
that you are that which experiences,
in the same way I do when I write these words,
when I write them from the experience
of being that which experiences.

Maybe you feel the taste of, fragrance of,
feel the vibrations of something
that you cannot describe with words,
namely that you are that which experiences.
Surely it has a taste, a fragrance,
a vibration that you recognize.
I suggest that you do recognize,
because you, too, are that which experiences.
You feel that you are what experiences when you read these words,
just as I feel that I am what experiences when I write these words.

From this, it is possible to see that you and I are the same,
that you and I are that which experiences.
What is experienced does not change what we are.
Nothing can change what we are.
Not our history, not what we are experiencing now,
not what we are going to experience.
What we are, is both the beginning and the end,
alpha and omega.
What we are, therefore has neither beginning nor end,
but what we are, is both the beginning and end of everything.

❦

Why I write – or not

I don't have any world view
or explanatory model for reality.
If I say or write something,
it has nothing to do with reality.
If you are of the opinion that
this is why I am writing, it is in you,
and I cannot be held accountable for it.

I simply am, and I experience.
What I experience or not
does not affect what I am.
For some reason
that I don't understand,
I am reporting from experience.
And I do not succeed at all.

There is always something in the way.
The wrong word, the intellect interferes,
misunderstandings due to culture,
age, background, gender…
I have never really believed
that I would ever succeed.

But still, it flows out of me,
trying to describe or report from
what is irrefutably True.
This is simultaneously liberating,
because I really don't have anything else to write.
Then I'd rather be completely silent.
And then, lo and behold:

Truth speaks.

Chapter 1

Birth

The beginning of this journey is a birth that is not physical. Often and jokingly, Kierkegaard's words are cited: *Life can only be understood backwards; but it must be lived forwards* – but it was surely not written as a joke, because this is actually how I feel nowadays. A decennium ago, something began to dawn on me, and a process began, a process I could call a birth, in the sense that only now did I realize what my earthly life and my person really always was and is. Again, this is most likely nothing unique, many feel this way, in what is called the autumn years. What I came to see was so revolutionary, though, that when I look at it in the rearview mirror, I call it a kind of birth.

The baby Mischa was taught that he was something **other** than his parents and siblings, something other than the world, and perhaps this was absolutely necessary – but now, I have the favor to discover that which was the baby and the writing of this, and that which is reading this, and the whole world! That I am that which experiences everything – **and** everything that is experienced!

Drama is the beginning…

Summer 2011. On a small village party, I end up sitting across a very experienced theatre person from Åland, who tells me about her time in the world of theatre, both as director and actor. After listening to her a good while, I comment her story.

—"I would never be able to play a character in a play – I have never been able to be anything else than myself."

—"Ha!" she replies quickly, —"If you were to play a character in a play, you would see and bring out things in yourself that you don't even know that you have!"

I take it as a challenge, in all secrecy. And begin contemplating…

One year later, I join a small beginner's theatre group in the ancient youth house, and in the summer of 2013, I have a role in a play for the first time in my life – as Smirnov in Anton Tjechov's play *The Bear*.

Before I enter the stage, I stand behind the backdrop, eagerly waiting for my cue. My heart is racing, blood pressure rising, and it feels both wonderful and scary. I figure that the worst that can happen is that I faint, and that the play has to be postponed. But, in the moment that I take one step out from the backdrop and meet the eyes of the audience, it feels as though I **am** Smirnov – and I do and say what he would do and say in the context of what is happening in the script, on stage. All this happens so naturally and without thinking about my own person or the palpitations. The permissive openness for and receptivity to what is played out feels like a large vacuum of love that sucks it all in from the stage – not a passive emptiness, on the contrary, an active receptivity of an infinite "energy field". And in this field, I feel a freedom that I have never felt before, to just be what I am – and right now, I am Smirnov. Of course, these words are written after the fact, so I don't think like this when I play the part, I just flow with what is happening, and in this flow, the only thing that can happen happens, given the conditions of the played character – what the other characters say and do, the clothes I wear, the props, everything in Smirnov's world right now – and the result is what we can call the play *The Bear*. But when it happens, it is surely Now!

The Bear is the beginning of a few years in the world of theatre for me, through four larger productions and several smaller ones that I put up myself. Together with my daughter and a friend, both having theatre experience, we then try to put up a play that we wrote ourselves, a fairly large production, but the financing doesn't work out, so it doesn't happen. But we do get a taste of making videos when we make a few short promotional trailers for our play. Then we buy some more film equipment and make four other shorts together with a few other friends.

Well, drama… To play a character. What happened to me in the play *The Bear* still happens when I act. When it comes to the acting itself, there is not a big difference between having a live audience or a camera in front of me. In the part, I am it, and what I do and say in the part is as natural as when I go shopping in the store or talk to people at work.

I seem to take this playing a part "one step further" than what I have heard of before. *If you were to play a character in a play, you would see and bring out things in yourself that you don't even know that you have!* said the woman at the table. Now I have experienced what it is like to play many different parts, with many different attributes, and also how it is received in an audience. But when I go shopping in the store or talk to people at work, is that not also a part, a role? Everything I do and say in my everyday role, is that not also practiced, learned, and conditioned by everything that has been and is my context, what the others say and do, the clothes I wear, and how all that dictates, directs me to do what I do and say in my everyday role? What is it that tells me, directs me to do what I do and say in my everyday role? And does it have to be in a certain way, in the usual way, "like I have always done it before"?

This is how I contemplate. From an early age, I am used to questioning conditioned ways to think and act, and now I question things in my own life, things that are learned and conditioned, and what my role actually is, and what it could look like if I really understood that.

Just like the actor does not change, is neither aggrandised nor diminished, neither wins nor loses anything of himself when he plays a certain role, it soon becomes obvious to me that even when my everyday role changes, what I really am does not change.

The imagination is not a state: it is the human existence* itself.

William Blake (1757–1827)

Toward the end of 2013, it
becomes clear that my
partner and I have been
on quite different paths
since we first met, even
though I had imagined it
to be the same path.

This comes as a minor
shock to me, and it starts a
period of introspection,
where nights and mornings
are filled with reading
books and on the internet
while the others are slee-
ping.

Music means a lot to me.
When I listen to *The
Dream Within* from the
movie *Final Fantasy – The
Spirits Within*, tears are
flowing and it feels as
though the sorrow of the
whole world pours over
me. I write the following,
just to get it out of me.

Where is this world?

The world where we love each other
where we have open hearts
open for each other and each others' needs

Why don't we just begin believing
and let our faith lead

Let go
be free
dare to be free

None of us want to see anyone suffer
or be without love

What separates us from each other?
Can we not see what that is, together
and decide together
that we have had it
so that we leave everything that separates us
and run toward everything that unites us

You know
they are near you
they who need you
what you can give
run, hurry there
you will be welcomed, naturally
don't be afraid

Run to your neighbor, your beloved, your child
hurry to each other
for we are surely the same
surely we are the same

Where is the world
where we can live
in harmony and delight?

Film fascinated me since childhood. During my introspection at the end of 2013, I watch the movie *Total Recall* (2012), in which Matthias (Bill Nighy) questions Hauser (Colin Farrell), and Matthias says something that really takes a hold on me. It begins my own search for what I really am.

Hauser: I want to remember.
Matthias: Why?
Houser: So I can be myself, be who I was.
Matthias: It is each man's quest to find out who he truly is, but the answer to that lies in the present, not in the past. As it is for all of us.
Houser: But the past tells us who we've become.
Matthias: The past is a construct of the mind. It blinds us. It fools us into believing it. But the heart wants to live in the present. Look there. You'll find your answer.

Something very unusual and strange happens to me soon after, when I am in a line, ordering pizza, with a couple of friends. A few people who I don't know come into the place, and one of them walks right up to me with determined steps, stops right in front of me, looks me straight into my eyes and says:

Can you remember what you were,
before the world told you
what you should be?

He then goes back to his friends, without saying anything else, and without looking at me again. My friends have seen what happened, and they are just as surprised as I am.

I have not met him, neither before nor after what happened, but later I am told about who he is, so it was not an angel or imaginary person.

What he asked me stayed with me for a long time, and one day, much later, I am able to look it up on the internet, and it turns out it is a quote from something that Charles Bukowski allegedly said or wrote. I don't know any more about Charles, but this quote really landed well in me, regardless of how or why it was said by the unknown friend in this way.

It starts to dawn on me that "the past is a construct," and if I look there, I will not find out what I am, because I am what I am now, not then. And that which experiences both my memories and the now, is what I am. Now.

As though in a meditative* state, completely focused on the experience of being, I sit for a few years, for long periods, many hours, with many texts from authors, lecturers, poets, philosophers*, and mystics* – all the while everyday life flows by in its usual pace.

Researchers and scientists like Susan Blackmore, Albert Einstein, Donald Hoffman, Bernardo Kastrup, Peter Russell, Rupert Sheldrake, and several others pass by on my computer screen, as well as philosophers and mystics like Adyashanti, Erik Baret, Werner Erhard, Jeff Foster, Dorothy Hunt, Jac O'Keeffe, Francis Lucille, Rupert Spira, Allan Watts, Ken Wilber, and many more.

When the recent philosophers point to old texts by Krishnamurti, Omar Khayyám, Nisargadatta, Ramana Maharshi, Rumi, Tagore, and others, I read them with great surprise: What thousands of years old texts, many philosophers, and scientists seem to point to, is the same thing, and something very obvious.

My search for what I really am, is no longer directed outward to matter or the world, neither to the past, but "inward" to whatever it is that is experiencing it all, now – even the very searching and the one searching! What is it that is on "this side" of experience?

A human being is a part of a whole, called by us "universe," a part limited in time and space. He experiences himself, his thoughts and feelings as something separated from the rest… a kind of optical delusion of his consciousness*.

. . .

This delusion is a kind of prison for us, restricting us to our personal desires and to affection for a few persons nearest to us. Our task must be to free ourselves from this prison by widening our circle of compassion to embrace all living creatures and the whole of nature in its beauty.

. . .

The true value of a human being can be found in the degree to which he has attained liberation from the self.

. . .

We shall require a substantially new manner of thinking, if mankind is to survive.

. . .

[We] know that the distinction between past, present and future is only a stubbornly persistent illusion.*

Albert Einstein (1879–1955)

It may sound academic or complicated to be on this kind of "exploration," but it really is not. On the contrary, because **to experience** is what we are most used to ever since birth – we really haven't been doing anything else than precisely experience! So to explore **what it is** that experiences cannot be strange or something that needs to be described or explained by certified philosophers or others in academia or science.

I hold fast to what Rupert Spira said: "To understand the world, it is a good idea to first understand **that which experiences** it."

In the first years on this journey, I meet a few others who are interested in these topics. We ask questions and taste the answers, test and investigate ourselves in experiences, and research *Being* in many different ways; in creating music, dance, theatre, film, websites, texts, etc.

To begin understanding and feeling what it is that experiences is so fascinating that I feel like an infatuated teenager. I can sit still, just feeling, experiencing, both sorrow and pain, as well as joy and pleasure – and simultaneously be unfathomably content with what I am, that which experiences, on this side of what is experienced, always the same, neither gaining nor losing anything, and fundamentally unaffected by what is experienced.

I also discover that there already is an expression for this: **Equanimity**, defined as a "composure which is undisturbed by experience".

About existence

If no thing, nothing, can come from nothing – it then follows that no thing, nothing can disappear, go back to nothing. Something we all know really exists, maybe the only existing, namely Consciousness, can neither be created nor disappear!

Does the brain produce consciousness?

What is this direct experience appearing in? Witnessing awareness is already present before the causal process even arises. So these processes cannot possibly cause the witnessing awareness that preceded it. These processes can't cause that to which they appear. It was already there!

Goode, Greg. *The Direct Path: A User Guide.* Non-Duality Press, 2012.

Consciousness is reality

– If there is only one reality, everything's reality, then consciousness of reality must be only one.
– Why?
– Because consciousness must then be this only reality.

Thirst

Do not look for water.
Look for thirst.

Rumi (1207-1273)

In my eagerness to try and communicate and reflect how I now feel, how it is actually fully possible – and also very practical – to see the world this way, some friends and I write many texts together, make a website for them, write scripts for plays we can put up, later on we make videos, and we have many meetings where I live, bathing in experiences that clearly show how we can shift our focus from **what** we see, to **how** we see. Here are a few examples of those texts:

Any paradigm based on the idea that the world is composed of separate material things, and therefore that some matter has developed its own consciousness, will lead to a failure in fulfilling the apparent desires and needs of these seemingly separate conscious entities, and will eventually fall. Any concept inside such a paradigm, will eventually serve against its thinkers, and lead to suffering; lack of love, peace, and happiness.

Inevitably, as proven throughout history, such paradigms lead to the belief that one apparent entity or one population is better or worth more than another, at which time we see the emergence of aggression and exploitation, whether on a personal or national level. Again, suffering ensues.

All suffering, then, if honestly investigated, leads us to a truth of another paradigm. A truth that all humans long to embrace, in fact a truth that is always shining through even the most materialistic and dualistic world view – because in ever present and timeless consciousness, there is no resistance to even dualism or materialism. Reality simply complies and conforms to any and all world views, no matter how "unreal".

A paradigm based on the idea (and actually experienced reality, if investigated honestly and rigorously) that the world is composed of the same consciousness, which itself is ultimate fulfillment, in and by which all seemingly material forms manifest, cannot fail. Within such a paradigm, all concepts align with its inherent fulfillment; love, peace, and happiness.

We all long to be one with God.

We all long to be one with each other.

We are.

We have simply forgotten it
and mistaken our identity
with something that seems separate.

Let us remember.

Looking down on the stars

One autumn evening, we lay in the grass silently, filled with wonder, looking up at the stars. My daughter says that we can see it as in fact looking **down** on the stars.

It takes me a while, but all of a sudden, things turn for me, everything flips! The planet is now lying on my back and I look down on the stars. And I feel it in my whole body.

In space, there is no up or down, of course. Direction is based on a particular perspective – and it can change!

(My) Declaration of Love

I love you!

I really love each and every one I have ever come in contact with! From when I looked out from my mother's womb to now and forever, you have told me, shown me, reminded me of the only reliable thing: I am, I live, I am life!

To all who I once thought did something mean to me, I can deeply from my heart say:

Thank you for being! Of course you are forgiven, because it was not what you did that meant something, but that you helped me understand that I am life!

To all who I thought did something nice to me, I can deeply from my heart say:

Thank you for being! Of course I was temporarily happy for what you did, but what truly meant something, was that you helped me understand that I am life!

How can I therefore hold any one of you higher or lower, better or worse that any other? Now, the grace to live life with every one and all, is too great to even contain the thought of comparing or judging. We and all others are life, all together.

What I love is life and love. Not the things or people that life and love contains, but life and love itself. But since I absolutely cannot find any separation, no border, between life and life's content – I can only love you and everyone, and everything that has been and is life and love.

We are forever woven together, we are all one and the same "being" of life. It is impossible to make any meaningful separation, because – from when my body was my mother's and father's body, to when events and activities brought us together in this magnificent fabric of life – everything is connected. So I can neither remove or add, nor change anything, not even find a cause or effect for anything – but we have been and are woven together, completely and fully, and I cannot separate myself from anything or any one in this fantastic and motley fabric.

"

And actually: Even if I at times tried to isolate myself, those efforts were also in the fabric of life – which never resists being woven! Why, then, should I?

At the same time, I am so deeply grateful for how you love me! Life, you and I, in the same whirling dance, have met, acted, cooperated, and interacted. Completely without you or me ever thinking about it, we were one and the same exuberant life together! And absolutely regardless of what we did or what happened.

Thank you for being! For having been and being in my life, regardless of whether I thought of it as good or bad, right or wrong! You have contributed to the greatest revelation, insight and gratitude: That I love you, that I love life, and that life loves us!

Now, I can only continue to be what I know I am: Love. Unfathomable and wordless, time- and space-less love. Nothing needs to change, life in love never ends, even if our actions and bodies do, when that time comes. All I want and am, is to love and be so close, that we are always reminded that we are one, one life, one love.

I cannot refrain from giving you my favorite quote, which has come to mean so much to me. Maybe to you, too, beloved.

Being

Exuberant is existence, time a husk.
When the moment cracks open,
ecstasy leaps out and devours space;
love goes mad with the blessings,
like my words give.

Why lay yourself on the torturer's rack
of the past and the future?
The mind that tries to shape tomorrow
beyond its capacities will find no rest.

Be kind to yourself, dear – to our innocent follies. Forget any sounds or touch you knew that did not help you dance.

You will come to see that all evolves us.

Rumi (1207-1273)

Knowledge

The mind's knowledge of anything
is only as good as its knowledge of itself.
Therefore, there is no higher knowledge
than to know the nature of the mind.

Rupert Spira (1960-)

I feel like newly hatched into this new seeing on the world, and most of it now seems to actually be in a way that is 180° from what I was told by others since birth.

Everything I experience, everything that changes, is experienced in what I am – even my mind and body are experienced, and they change, too.

I cannot find any distance between what I am and what I experience. Both the song of the birds and the pain from the mosquito bite happens in what I am. As well as the friend I talk to on the phone or meet in town. And the phone. And the town.

What the world looks like, now seems to depend more on **how** I see, than on **what** I see.

It feels so new and wonderful to see the world this way. It is as though it relates to how I see it, and conforms to how I see it, regardless of how I saw it before. When I see it as something that appears in what I am – and no longer I who appear in it – I feel the same openness for what the world is, as well as its openness to how I see it. Hard to explain...

In this new seeing, I am filled with such wonderment and reverence for both large and small things in life, as they are no longer something outside or separate from what I am. The texts of the old mystics now become something I embrace and feel connected to.

That which experiences

That which experiences matter and objects, must be at least as real or more real than what is experienced – but from direct experience, we know that it is more real: Consciousness.

Everything in Consciousness

Everything experienced has always been or happened in consciousness.

Nothing experienced has ever been or happened outside consciousness.

Nothing outside of consciousness is ever experienced.

Everything is, happens, and is experienced in and by consciousness.

Consciousness, the only reality, is what the world – all things including us human beings – consist of!

We are the same

In fact, my soul and yours are the same,

You appear in me, I in you,

We hide in each other.

Rumi (1207-1273)

Guest

I am merely a guest
born in this world,
to know the secrets
that lie beyond it.

Rumi (1207-1273)

The mind imposes its own limits on everything that it sees or knows, and thus all its knowledge and experience appear as a reflection of its own limitations. It is for this reason that scientists will never discover the reality of the universe until they are willing to explore the nature of their own mind.

Everything the mind knows is a reflection of its own limitations.

Rupert Spira (1960-)

A man travels the world over
in search of what he needs
and returns home to find it.

George A. Moore (1852-1933)

Realization is nothing new to be acquired. It is already there, but obstructed by a screen of thoughts. All our attempts are directed to lifting this screen and then realization is revealed.

Ramana Maharshi (1879-1950)

In the middle of the forest,
there's an opening
that can be found
only by the one who got lost.

Thomas Tranströmer (1931-2015)

I am water, I am beginning.
I was before the oaks, the grass,
and the flowers.
I was before the cattle that graze.
I was before hovering wing
and running foot.
I was before the bumblebees,
the bees and the birds.

I was before the sorrow and the joy.
I was before the weeping
and the laughter.
I was before the pain and the agony
and the anguish on earth.
I was before the human race.

Vilhelm Moberg (1898-1973)

Searching

Searching for myself, my true nature,
truth, happiness, answers…
Searching and longing, desiring to find…

This is why it is written:
"Desire is the beginning of suffering".
Not because that which I desire is wrong,
but because desire blinds me from seeing
that I already am what I am looking for.

I am you

At a distance
you only see my light.
Come closer
and know that I am you.

Rumi (1207-1273)

God

What is reality?

The world is illusory;

Brahman* alone is real;

Brahman is the world.

Ramana Maharshi (1879–1950)

The eye through which I see God is the same eye through which God sees me; my eye and God's eye are one eye, one seeing, one knowing, one love.

Meister Eckhart (1260 –1328)

Silence is the language of god,
all else is poor translation.

Rumi (1207-1273)

God sleeps in the rock, dreams in the plant,
stirs in the animal, and awakens in man.

Ibn Arabi (1165–1240)

In most religions that I have looked at, primarily Christianity, I now see that when they talk about deity, they point to what is always the same, the origin of everything, contains everything and every experience, both "good and evil," is time- and spaceless, etc. Since this is the definition of what we can call Consciousness, I see that when mystics from different religions speak of their "God," they are pointing to what I call Consciousness.

I find it absolutely incredible how the makeup of nature itself reflects what it appears in, the True, the Creator... In Ibn Arabi's text above we can see how:
- the rock represents deep sleep. Empty, but still consisting of God/the dreamer.
- the plants represent dreaming. Many things, but no interaction, but still consisting of God/the dreamer.
- the animals represent lucid dreaming. Many things, interaction with them, but still consisting of God/the dreamer.
- man represents awakeness, when he realizes that he himself and everything is the same, in the same God/dreamer, in which everything appears and borrows its reality from.

Hidden deity

According to an old Hindu legend, there was once a time when all human beings were gods, but they so abused their divinity that Brahma, the chief God, decided to take it away from them and hide it in a place where it could never be found. In order to find the best spot, however, he needed to hold a council of the gods to help him decide.

"Let's bury it deep in the earth," said the gods.

Brahma answered, "No, that will not do, because humans will dig into the earth and find it."

The gods replied, "Okay, let's sink it in the deepest ocean then."

But Brahma said, "No, not there, for they will learn to dive, and they will find it."

Then the gods said, "What about the highest mountain top, out in the farthest corner of the earth?"

But again Brahma replied, "No, that will not do either, because they will eventually climb every mountain, scale every peak, search every hidden cave and once again find and take up their divinity."

The rest of the gods were exasperated. They threw up their arms in surrender. "There is no place!" they hollered. "The humans will proliferate, and they will find it anywhere we put it."

Brahma was quiet for a time. He thought long and deep. Finally, he looked up at the rest of the gods, a knowing twinkle in his eye. "Here is what we shall do," he said. "We will hide their divinity deep down in the one place they will surely never look – the very center of their own being."

The rest of the gods rejoiced. Of course! It was the perfect place! They all formally agreed on it, and the deed was done.

Ages passed, and since that time, humans have been on a desperate and unending search, traveling every corner of the planet, digging, diving, climbing, and exploring – searching for the one thing they know they've lost, and just can't seem to find.

(Unknown)

Everywhere?

God is everywhere? But most of us believe that God is somewhere, and that we are somewhere else. But there is nowhere where God is not. Where we are, cannot be a bubble where God is not. Where we are, God is. There is no separation between us. All separation is illusory.

CHAPTER 2

Litmus test

A litmus test is used in chemistry to test the acidity of a substance. The concept "litmus test" is sometimes also used as a metaphor* that points to a simple and clear way of answering a question. One philosopher claimed "experience is the litmus text of reality," that is to say, if something can be experienced, it is real. I now begin to use the test this way, I let experience show me what is real. This test has worked very well so far, and it turns out that much of what I believed and thought earlier, simply was not real. **What** I think I experience ("the sun is warming me") need not be true (it is actually a hot stove that is warming me) – but the experience (of heat) is real.

I don't go to "retreats"

Possible scenario: I go to a retreat or a self-help conference, visit a guru or the like, and take everything I am with me. I experience things, and take everything I am with me when I return home.

The experiences do not change anything (even though it might feel like that for a while). The experiences are not equipped with any sort of power or energy that can change anything of what I am.

If any change happens, it happens exactly where I am, in me, and I actually cannot describe fully, not even to myself, why or how the change happened. And the change itself is also only an experience.

Inherent in the perspective of our culture, there seems to be a built-in belief that we are always insufficient in ourselves, and that we therefore need external aid to become better. And to feel sufficient in oneself can even be thought of as bad, wrong, egocentric, etc. "Self-sufficient" is often used in a derogatory sense in our language.

I feel that this perspective – because it is only a perspective – completely misses something true and fundamental: Whatever I am, it is here, in what I am, where everything is experienced. Change, too. And we don't need to talk about insufficiency. Not about self-sufficiency either, nor what is called egocentrism, self-centeredness, selfishness, etc.

Whatever I am, is by definition and in itself sufficient to experience everything that is experienced, and to be the only reality (as no other reality has actually ever been experienced, anyway). When I see this and act from this, what seems to happen is that the culturally conditioned perspective slowly but surely loses its importance, and the trust in what I am calms my whole being. In what I am, change can happen less affected by my own and others' perspectives. And then the change happens! All "by itself," in what I am.

The reality of everything

What exists, exists out of something – which is the definition of existence. Therefore, this something must be more real, more reliable and continuous, than what exists. So regardless of the existence of x, y, and z, it cannot affect this something. Therefore, this something must be the reality of everything. And since we are that which experiences what exists, we must be this one and the same reality.

Music and communication

The music is not in the computer, nor on the cd, nor in the phone,
not even in the sound waves that reach the eardrum.
The illusory separate and mechanical is not music.
Music is an experience in consciousness.
Consciousness, through the composer, turns out to be
the same consciousness that is me
when I listen to the composer's music.
Time- and space-less.
In the experience of music,
conceptual time and space collapses,
as well as every illusory separation.

The same goes for all communication with content, meaning, and intent,
expressions out of consciousness through our persons.
Consciousness gives rise to words in the mind,
the mind processes and influences,
affects the brain which affects nerves and muscles,
the mouth that forms sound waves,
which meet my eardrums, nerves, and mind,
meets the same consciousness in me, and I understand –
that we are one in what is expressed, communicated and understood.

The same goes for love. Or rather:
When we experience that we are one,
regardless whether it is in speech, music, or relationships,
it then is and consists of love, peace, and happiness.

– "Though I speak with the tongues of men and of angels,
and have not charity, I am become as sounding brass, or a tinkling cymbal."

1 Corinthians 13:1

Concept-less reality

In all activities where we seem to experience that we are one – music, art, nature, sex, etc, in the world of perception – when we seem to dissolve and lose ourselves, our identity and the concept of time and space, and where thought is secondary or stopped altogether, we are really only reminded of reality itself, we are not in a state, it is not the activity that produces an altered state:

We are reminded that we are one, and that there is no time or space, ever.

Only when the mind seemingly forgets that and identifies with our bodies, is the apparent world of time and space created through and by our perception and thought only.

Difficult…

That things are not the way I want
or have imagined that they should be,
can become more important to me
and be experienced as more difficult
than the consequence of them being as
they are.
If I don't resist how things are,
the difficulties and concerns with them
subside.

Silence

Silence is unceasing eloquence.
It is the best language.

Ramana Maharshi (1879–1950)

Opposite

The opposite of death is not life.
It is birth.

Knowledge

Man's chasing after knowledge, is in fact a chasing after a knowing of what we are: Consciousness. He has merely forgotten that. Consciousness is everything already, but when man forgets this, it becomes important to know as much as possible about every detail in the world.

Movement

When I experience motion,
say, when I travel in a car…
I can experience motion only if
I am a reference point that is still.

What I actually am,
is that reference point.
What I actually am,
is never in motion!

Motion can be experienced
only by what is still.
Motion is illusory in what I am –
stillness itself.

The character in the movie

Whatever the separate self is, it can be compared to a character in a movie.

What I am,
is the screen.

But actually, brutally honestly,
there is only the screen.

Thoughts

What I think about something
does not change anything,
except what I am thinking.

Thermostat

Just as a thermostat is not conscious and
cannot describe what it is like to be a
thermostat, my body is not conscious.
The sensations* of the body can only be
experienced in consciousness, which alone
can experience what it is like to have a
body – and what it is like to be
conscious… of itself.

Meet

When we meet
are we looking into each other's eyes?
No, into each other's pupils, the apple of
the eye.

The pupil is a hole,
so what emanates out from a hole?
What is exchanged between two holes,
when we meet?

Neither light nor matter.
We are the same emptiness,
filled with everything.

Does the mind die?

Mind is something that consciousness
manifests itself as. In mind, the
identification with a body, events, and
labels happens, and thus, an illusory ego is
formed.

When the body dies, mind does not.

But: That which in mind has identified
with a body, events, and labels – which
were never really true – keeps being not
true, and non-existent.

Mind, free from this identification,
carries on.

Everything we know, is known through
Awareness; therefore, our knowledge of
anything is only as good as our knowledge
of Awareness.

If we believe that Awareness is limited,
experience will appear in accordance with
that belief, as a succession of limited, finite
objects and selves.

If we understand that Awareness is eternal
and infinite, everything and everyone will
be revealed as such.

Rupert Spira (1960–)

What we long for is the space of
Awareness in which all longing takes
place.

In fact, it is even closer than that.

What we long for is itself taking the shape
of our longing.

Rupert Spira (1960–)

Ego?

Ego-death is nothing.

It is when I experience that I am one with
everything I experience, that I do not find
an ego.

To "kill the ego," is to realize this. And
experience!

See more?

Everything
is already here.
My wish
for things to be different
is also here.
Disappointment, too.

I see so little
of everything that is here.
Perhaps I can see more
and wish less.
Probably, no surely,
that is fully sufficient.

Spiritual?

If something is "spiritual,"
then it is something that
allows me to see what I am –
that I am Eternal Spirit
that through "the spiritual"
sees itSelf being me.
And everything else.
Independently of "the spiritual".

Reach You

Your longing for me
is my message to you.

All your attempts to reach me,
are in reality my attempts to reach You.

Rumi (1207-1273)

Is

That which is, never ceases to be;
that which is not,
never comes into existence.

Bhagavad Gita

Deviation

Just this nature of pure and total
consciousness is the ultimate essence of all
that exists… Treading a path to reach
what cannot be reached by treading
causes deviation; seeking to understand
conceptually that which cannot become
an object [of thought] causes the
hindrances that obstruct understanding…
seeking something and striving to obtain it
constitute deviation.

Namkhai Norbu (1938–2018)

Your confusion is not pathology, it is path. It has something to show you that clarity could never reveal. The nature of chaos is wisdom, but you must provide a home for it to receive its mysteries.

Your feeling of disconnection is not neurotic, it is intelligent. It has something to show you that oneness could never reveal. If you will allow it to unfold and illuminate – resisting the temptation to convert it via spiritual process – it will disclose an unmet doorway.

Your loneliness, your shakiness, and your fear are not mistakes. They are not obstacles on your path. They **are** the path. The freedom you are longing for will never be found in the eradication of the unwanted, but only in the love and the information it carries.

There are surges of somatic activity that contain very important information for your journey. If you will offer safe passage for the unknown aliveness, you will meet the messengers of illumination. Nothing is missing, nothing is out of place, and nothing need be sent away.

Yes, you may burn until you are translucent, but it is by way of this burning that your wholeness will be revealed.

Matt Licata

State-less

When I go from dream-less deep sleep to dreaming, and also from lucid dreaming to a waking state, what is it that "goes" then? What is it that always is, and "goes" through all states of the body and mind?

In the waking state, it is not the body that experiences, it is what I am that experiences the body, and that the body feels, senses things.

Dreams are dreamt by the mind, not by what I am. It is what I am that experiences that they are dreamed, and can tell us about them later.

Contact

The dreamed character – which appears in the mind of the dreamer – is in contact with the dreamer in a lucid dream.

In exactly the same way, we – who appear in consciousness – are in contact with consciousness, the same consciousness, right now.

Already

We know it already. The question is,
what does it mean?

When it so infinitely and beautifully
bubbles, simmers, vibrates…
wants up, out, forward…
When love in intoxication
wells up, overflows,
and only wants to embrace,
contain, erase borders.
Heal everything, without scars,
just become and be one.
As it already is.
I am there.
It is I.
I am it.

It is before thought.
And before everything.

As soon as I speak or do something,
it comes out as something else,
interpreted, misinterpreted, maybe it even hurts.
What Is, can be perceived as wrong,
when they only hear my rambling words.

We know that it is.
All attempts to reach it
only lead to suffering.
It is. We are. It. Already.
Now and always.
How could we forget?

Seen

For anything visible to be seen
there first needs to be a "receiver" that sees.
The form that is seen, appears in the receiver.
The infinitely thin "skin" between what is seen
and what is experienced in the "receiver,"
is what we call "the world".
The receiver is Consciousness, without limit,
and that which is seen and experienced in Consciousness
must therefore consist of what it appears in.

Matter

Matter cannot describe what it is like to be matter.
But we can definitely and precisely describe what it is like to be.
Therefore, what we really are cannot be or consist of matter.
Matter cannot be the origin of that which is not matter.

Find out

Before we say anything about
what the world we experience is or consists of,
it is expedient to first and thoroughly find out
what it is that experiences it.

No information in the world we experience,
can tell us what it is that experiences it,
what we are.

The only one who can find this out
and know it, is you.

Time and space

Time is what consciousness looks like, from the perspective of thought.
Space is what consciousness looks like, from the perspective of perception.

We do not experience objects with our consciousness.
Objects happen, they are events that are precipitated in the perception of mind.

The essence, the reality of objects – is consciousness.

Peel off

I cannot be something
that I am conscious of.

I am what is conscious.

If I peel off from this "me,"
everything that is not me;
what am I left with?

I am what is conscious –
Consciousness itself!

Waves

The wave's only destination
is to die,
to rediscover
that it is ocean.

Waves that are born and die,
are always ocean.

See myself

As little as the eye can see itself,
thoughts, feelings, sensations,
and perceptions
can see themselves.

That which sees them is what I am.
Consciousness.

Flower

The garden,
in tranquility and harmony,
was given a flower.

In the same way,
I was given a body.

I experience…

In every situation, I can ask myself:
"What am I experiencing now?"

If I have a thought about something
that I claim gives me or creates a feeling
of loneliness, anger, or desolation,
I ask myself "what am I experiencing
now?"

Whatever that is, I can answer that I
experience sorrow, loneliness, events, etc.

But really, what am I experiencing?
Sounds, other sensations of the senses,
perceptions, thoughts, and feelings.

They cannot be me, because I,
what I really am, experience them.

What I am, does not protect me
from experiencing.

But the freedom in being
what everything appears in,
is experienced in,
means that I am not damaged.

Ego-death

It is not possible to live in the now
without the ego "dying".

The ego can never live in the now,
but only in the past or the future.

Simulation

Since there's absolutely no guarantee that my bodily senses, thoughts, perceptions, and emotions accurately represent reality (it's rather guaranteed that they **don't**)… but I obviously **am** real – I **must** be something more than and encompassing whatever my bodily senses, thoughts, perceptions and emotions "do" or tell me.

Whatever is and always has been the **same** as whatever I am, must be what I am. Not much, granted – but it is what everyone totally agrees with: **I am**. And "your" **I am**, is obviously the same as "my" and "everyone" else's **I am**, because all the "differences" I can think of, have **not** been and are never the **same**.

What my bodily senses, thoughts, perceptions and emotions "do" and tell me, is therefore more of a "simulation".

Dreams

Dreams are what they are and work the way they do, because they are – just as everything natural – a "reflection" of and analogous to what is true. The dreamed character that doesn't know that it is and consists of the dreamer's mind, is analogous to the seemingly separate person in its waking state, where the person doesn't know that it is and consists of Consciousness.

Just as the dreamed character consists of the mind of the dreamer that dreams it,
our awake characters consist of Consciousness that "dreams" them.

Just as the dreamed character returns to and dissolves in the dreamer who wakes up,
our awake characters return to and dissolve in Consciousness.

The same

Those relationships we've had,
that love we wanted,
how the same it always is,
how the same I am.
And you.

Now is

I cannot change the now.
Not escape from now, not leave it.
What is, only is.
If I doubt what is,
want to change the now, flee from now,
it is also what is.

Everything happens in me
and consists of me.
Devoid of liability*
and cause and effect.

See the same

The fact that we see the same things in the world
says nothing about the things' or the world's existence or reliability,
it says that we are the same, which experiences the same forms
in the same Consciousness that are us.

Mirror image

I happen to see the reflection of my face on the computer screen while I'm listening to something, completely merged with what I'm listening to.

In this merging, there is no subject or object, I am solely the experience of understanding.

Seeing the reflection of my face is so comical that I begin to laugh out loud.

I experience how consciousness can limit itself and appear as a limited form, and that identification with this form can happen.

It would be correct to say about the reflection "That is I," because the form consists solely of consciousness.

But to say that I am a delimited object, a body that is the substance of and producing my experience, would be both naive and arrogant – naive because my direct experience is the other way around, that consciousness appears as a form, and arrogant because it would be so absurd that a body with a brain would originate the experience of this merging in consciousness, a merging that demonstrates my time- and space-less existence, completely independent of form!

More laughing out loud

I start laughing out loud again.

When my thoughts no longer reside in the past or the future, I only think about what is right now. And when the ideas about what I see no longer stand between me and what I see, I do not experience any boundary. Events just happen. Things just appear.

When I experience that I am one with existence in this fashion, I can still perceive it in many different ways. But right now, I perceive it as something laughable, free and welcome, just as it is.

Imagine that I get to experience all this! Thankfully, and incredibly comically, when I see it like that.

What it feels like

I am on an adventure with a friend, and we do something that is difficult and hard; we walk on small beams, high up on skyscrapers, hundreds of feet above the ground. I tense up and things don't go so well because I am scared.

But the friend shows me that it's all pretend, it's an illusion that we are so high up, it's actually just a film projected onto the floor from underneath!

I laugh and relax, and everything goes much easier and better.

Such is the realization about what reality is.

We are now

What we are, is now.
We all know – also intellectually – that now is,
but the intellect cannot be in it.
We know that the intellect, thought,
resides only in the past or the future.
So whatever now is, it is where we are.
And that we therefore are not our intellect.

So close

What you seek is so near you that there is no place for a way.

Nisargadatta Maharaj (1897–1981)

We are I

So you want to explore the very smallest,
in order to maybe find a structure,
a frequency, a principle,
that is the origin of everything?
You look for a song of truth in there?
I am the song. Listen!

So you want to travel to the very largest
in order to maybe find a beginning,
an intelligence, or maybe life,
the true origin of everything?
You want to find a creator there?
I am the creator. See!

In a universe that you claim
begins with and consists of solely matter,
you are looking in all directions for
beginning, meaning, and intelligence.
I am!
That.

Thoroughly, feel what is searching.
In a universe that you are
inseparable from,
that is you.
I am you.
We are I.

Relating

The world relates exactly
to how I think.
Not the other way around.

When I see objects

I identify with the body
because "it is I who see objects".

I do not identify with objects, because
they are "something other than I".
But actually…
I am both.

Because if there were nothing to see,
I would not be that which sees
or experiences seeing.

Another example:
A circle cannot be a circle if there is not
both an outside and an inside.

In the same way, everything is connected
and is actually something that
consciousness experiences.

As a matter of fact, everything is in
consciousness, not the other way around.

Resistance

When a will or wish happens,
to change the content of experience,
identification has happened,
and in it, there is an idea about
or belief in lack
and a resistance to what is.

Formlessness

It is formlessness that is, always.
It is experienced in deep sleep when the mind has stopped, quieted down.
It is the formlessness we want.
We feel a strong desire for the deep sleep,
but no strong desire to leave it,
because we wake up "by ourselves,"
or by mechanically set alarms.

It is in this formlessness we take any form.
We soar through dimensionlessness,
and go into and experience any dimension in the dream.
But we are the dimensionlessness.

It is not the way we thought,
that we go from the most conscious and awake state
and then go "down" into and become limited in the dream,
and then further "down" in unconscious deep sleep.

No, our natural state is not the waking state. On the contrary.
When we leave our natural state in deep sleep
and then dive down into the dream, we are limited in time.
When we dive down into the waking state, there is more limitation,
in the three dimensions of the awake state,
to a body that may be weak or sick.
Here, it is possible to believe that life is so small and limited.
But no! On the contrary!

Shining

I know that I in no way depend on the experienced euphoria.
I know that it occurs in my body-mind,
when the remembrance of my true nature is strong.

Just as fully, I know, every time, that if the euphoria were to cease,
I do not cease – I shine with the same light,
in, as, and through every experience.

Itself

It is easy to realize that the music we become one with, is not or consists not of sound waves, but nothing other than Consciousness.

It is a little harder to realize that it is Consciousness that loves itself then.

It is most difficult to realize that this whole experience of being an illusory separate person, including the listening to music, all feelings and thoughts, and this text being read now, is and consists of the same Consciousness. That loves itself.

That is what we are – Love.

Why not now?

A view, known or not,
that permeates our culture is:

You can become…
or will become…
happy…
later.

I wonder:
Why not now?

Silence is golden?

In silence,
we are all equal.

The same.

This does not change
when we speak.

Seems like…

It can seem like I can think myself out of the direct experience, that I can "leave the now" that way.

Reversely, it is possible to believe that it is necessary to stop thinking in order to go into the direct experience, to be present in the now.

But none of this is correct, both are simply perceptions and thoughts.

Direct experience and presence in the now is always. And often, apparent forgetfulness of this fact happens. As well as the direct experience of thoughts.

And the ceasing of thoughts.

Communication

Never ever
has anyone communicated
an experience
of anything,
to anyone.

Yet, all we know,
and all we are,
is only experiencing.
Therefore,
communication does not
do anything for what we are.

Shared experiencing,
as it seems to be,
is all there is,
and all we can be –
as we always are.

Talking to myself

I can see it for what it is,
all this.
But I can also go into it.
And it seems so real then.
But when I see it for what it is,
I see only Myself,
as this,
with no border,
no separation,
no identification,
just a multitude of colors and sounds,
in Me.

It is so intimate
and close to Me,
that I cannot but say
that it is Me.
This is Me, everything.
It's completely overpowering to the mind,
so I just leave the mind to itself.
It definitely does not define me,
and every night, it ceases to operate,
in deep sleep.
So I will just yield
to the seeing that this is Myself,
manifesting as this.

With more experience
it gets harder and harder
to go back into all this.
But I can do it.
As I'm in it,
watching it from "my" perspective,
it seems so small
and almost boring.

Seeing it for what it is
takes the edge off it,
that personal edge,
and everything is
so seamlessly enjoyable,
completely void of valuation.

I can really tell
that there is a play going on.
Going into the play,
and becoming that very familiar role –
although everywhere I look, I see Myself –
I am still both the actor and the role.

Back in the role,
I can say a lot of things,
none of which would be True,
because it is not seeing things as they are,
it is seeing things the way they appear.
But I can be that character in the play,
or not. Or both.
Yet, everywhere I look, I see myself.

Alone?

I am always alone,
but never feel lonely.

Boundless beauty

The appreciation of, say, reading a poem
is a confirmation that I have already
experienced the boundless beauty
that the poem reminds me of.

Love gets all the glory

Something happens,
and the euphoria subsides?
Eventually, I blame
what has happened
for the euphoria subsiding.
—"If only this or that
had not been
or had not happened,
Love would have…"

But I am thrown back into the memory
of the euphoria of being Love itself,
and how it is unconditional.
And I realize that my thoughts –
however well they describe
what has happened –
are only thoughts
that are not the euphoria,
and even less the Love.

So the Love that "endures all things"
is not disturbed by the thoughts at all.
It doesn't matter
what the thoughts are –
they are the role,
and Love
is playing that role.
And Love gets the glory,
not the role.

The intellect experienced

I know that I am. Here.
The intellect that is experienced
cannot comprehend this,
because what is here
experiences the intellect.

What is here
makes the intellect possible.
So the intellect cannot understand
what it is made of.
The intellect is made of my Self,
experiencing it.

So in this way,
I am not my intellect;
I am experiencing it.

I who see

I am what sees.
Not what is seen.
Whatever is seen,
is not what I am.

Regardless of what
or how I see,
or do not see,
I am always the same.

What I see
is limited by the mind.
So whatever I see,
is in reality made of mind.

What I see always changes in the mind,
but since I am
that which sees the changes,
what I am is… unchangeable.

To be everything

To be all things that are experienced,
feels like so incredibly much more –
so exciting, touching, intimate,
and deeply satisfying –
than to be only thinking and
talking about them,
as though they were separate.

This is how it feels for the separate mind,
because what experiences
and what is experienced
already and always is and consists of
the same Consciousness
that we consist of.

When I see what it is
to be all the experienced things,
I also see that I can
refrain from perceiving this fact and
start thinking and talking about them –
which does not change this fact, though.

To be music

Listen to a musician,
and feel how obvious this is…

…to see how the musician is all his notes,
not just the notes you hear right now,
but every note,
that has been played, are played now,
and will be played later.

This is one way of seeing it.
In the same way, you can see it as
when I hear the notes now,
I am the musician,
who is all the notes.

It can now be attributed to the musician's
seemingly separate body-mind
that notes are conveyed
to my seemingly separate body-mind
that is listening.

But in the experience
of both the playing and listening,
there is no division,
they are actually the same.
Which we are.

Alone

I am not hearing notes – I hear music.
I am not seeing pixels on a screen –
I see a movie.
I am not perceiving objects –
I am experiencing.

I am conscious of the experience,
and I am also conscious of
that I am conscious of it,
so therefore I must be Consciousness
that is conscious of itSelf.

The music, the movie, and the objects,
and everything I experience,
is therefore my Self,
experiencing my Self.
Alone, all one.

Miracles

I do not believe in miracles outside of me.

I see that everything is miracles in me.

Why?

I can imagine all the possibilities
of why and how I am sitting right here,
all imaginable possibilities of…
all the wonderful and all the miserable,
from the wisest to the most idiotic,
from the most merciful to the cruelest,
… that made me sit here.

But oh, how surprising!
I know and feel that
this imagining of all the possibilities,
and each individual possibility,
and all their qualities,
is happening in this seeing
that I am speaking from now.

The questions "why?" and "how?"
therefore have no validity,
they have erased themselves.
I alone am left,
sitting here.

Impatience

My impatience
tells me that
I already am
the peace I feel
when I get what I want –
regardless if I get
what I want
or not.

Old saying

"I am not what you think I am.
You are what you think I am."

Unknown

So true!

Question?

In the same moment that a question
appears, it is possible to see it –
and everything else that is seen –
as part of the movie that appears on the
screen that I am.

Invaluable

What I Am
cannot be valued.
What I Am
experiences all valuation,
but in mySelf,
I am invaluable.

What Is

What I see is not **what Is**.
It is only what **what Is** looks like.
And it is nothing else than what
what Is looks like.

And what **what Is** looks like
doesn't matter.
What Is matters.

What is
is what sees,
and not what is seen.

My fallible neighbor

It is so easy to feel hurt and react
to someone angrily telling me
that there is something wrong with me or my behavior,
that I could say:
–"Well, you are not infallible,
so what right to you have to tell me that?"

I can easily turn this around.

Before I angrily tell someone
that there's something wrong with him or his behavior,
I can ask myself:
–"Hang-on! I would want someone who is angry with me
to realize that he's not infallible,
and that he therefore has no right to scold me –
so why would I scold this guy, then?"

In all this, there is a kind of permission
to be fallible,
which I would like to enjoy,
but do I want to allow others to be fallible, too?
I believe so.
And in this way, I love my neighbor as myself.

Power?

To ascribe an event some inherent power to make me happy or peaceful,
is the same as ascribing an object or person such power.

Events, objects, and persons come and go,
and they are experienced in and by what is not affected
by neither events, objects, nor persons.

Rejection?

If I reject someone because I don't tolerate what he's done, I am rejecting something in me that I don't tolerate, and then I'm not likely to accept it in myself – and the intolerance of others continues.

If I accept someone, regardless of what he's done, I have accepted and understood what I didn't tolerate in myself – and in this acceptance, intolerance ceases.

If it was my best friend who did the same thing, would I reject my friend then? If not, why would I reject the other? If I had done the same thing, would I reject myself then? If not, why would I reject the other?

Examples:
He takes up too much space when he feels ignored, but I know that this feeling cannot be compensated by taking up too much space. Do I feel ignored? I can understand that this would feel unbearable. If I instead see and expe-rience that I am that which sees, and understand the identification with "the ignored one" – neither the identi-fication nor the taking up too much space are needed any longer. And the rejection has ceased.

He does not show respect for others in practical matters, in an ongoing self-fulfilling prophecy about feeling worthless. Do I feel worthless? I can understand that this would feel unbearable. If I instead see and understand that I am that which is everything and that I am invaluab-le, and that which experiences all valuation, and I un-derstand the identification with "the worthless" – neither the identification nor the self-fulfilling prophecy are nee-ded any longer. And the rejection has ceased.

Dislike?

My dislike of someone's behavior says nothing about that person, and actually nothing about the behavior in itself either.

My dislike is of something in me. What I dislike is that something is evoked in me when I observe the behavior. A discomfort, a dislike is evoked by something that in itself is merely a possible behavior.

The possible behavior does not change what I am, it neither diminishes nor enlarges what I am, and therefore it needs neither my liking nor disliking.

When I realize this, the discomfort or dislike is not evoked in me when I see the behavior. One could say that I have accepted the behavior then – but it is much closer than that: I accept myself, as well as the possibility of such behavior, without any liking or disliking being evoked in me for that reason.

Not of this world

As I realize and feel that all that I am, and all that my world is,
is Consciousness expressing and experiencing itself as This,
I also confirm, deeply and humbly, with all of my being, that
everything that can be observed and experienced,
every form of Consciousness expressing and experiencing itself,
is not only exactly what I and my world are made of,
namely Consciousness expressing and experiencing itself,
but also one and the very same with, and inseparable from
everything that can be observed and experienced.

On the one hand…
This realization and confirmation can inform what seems to be my actions,
and thus my apparent actions become more aligned with
the Awareness of everything that I am,
completely naturally, and automatically.
Not because actions are preconceived or strived for,
but because actions happen naturally, automatically,
thus leaving absolutely no action to chance or predetermination,
pride or shame, good or bad discipline.
Informed actions are simply the Awareness that I am.

On the other hand…
This realization and confirmation can inform what seems to be my choices,
and thus my apparent choices become more aligned with
the Acceptance of the world that I am,
always available, and perfectly befitting.
Not because choices are mindfully or carefully made,
but because the choices that happen,
are those that are always available and perfectly befitting,
thus leaving absolutely no choice to ingenuity or stupidity,
pleasing or conniving, good or bad intent.
Informed choices simply are the Acceptance that I am.

Finally…
This realization and confirmation is not of this world,
but happens in it, without boasting itself,
without drawing attention* to itself,
without gain or loss for anyone,
as it only and always points to Truth,
that whatever I and this world may be,
it is Consciousness expressing and experiencing itself as This.

Integrity

I could have said: *—"You who cannot show respect for my integrity in a way that I am used to
or demand, to you I can say: When you rascals grew up, you might have learned to show respect
for integrity with a fart, something laughable at some party."*
Keep this thought…

Now note this:
This is not about how I am treated by them, this is about the keeping of my integrity.
By saying what I could have said to the rascals, I am pointing to something true, namely
integrity, something indivisible.

But how could I believe
that it is possible to lose, divide, or hurt
what is indivisible?
Integrity says more about what I am,
than what I have or can lose.

Pains

There are many kinds of pains
beyond the one that happens in my body,
when afflicted by or subjected to something that hurts.

Under one pain, I find that
"I thought I deserved better".
Under another pain I find that
"I have not resolved my own pain,"
maybe because I still think that I deserve better,
in turn maybe because I believe that it would hurt more
to give up the image of myself deserving better.
Under one pain I even find
the realization of the miserable state of the world,
and that there seems to be
no end in sight of all the suffering.
Or that whatever I do,
things don't seem to get better.

But no pain is permanent,
all pains cease, sooner or later.
All pains appear in what is permanent,
which itself cannot be defined
by neither pain nor pleasure,
that which from time to time contains
both pain and pleasure,
suffering and wellbeing.

Can I see and find, closest to me, furthest in,
on this side of all pain and all suffering,
this side of both pleasure and wellbeing…
myself, what I demonstrably, really,
and always am and always was?
That I am not what I see, hear, or touch,
I am not what I experience, nor what or how I feel?
And maybe I can even discover
that everything I experience
is so intimately close to what I am,
that there is no border or separation?

When I wake up on an ordinary morning, I have a memory of the experience of periods of deep sleep, when I was conscious about "nothing," or rather the absence of things (i.e. thoughts and dreams). But it is definitely an experience that I remember.

After this new kind of general anesthesia, though, I have no memory at all from when I was under. Before the anesthetic (propofol) has an effect, there is one "frame in my movie" that contains voices and the lights in the ceiling, and on the next "frame" a voice that says "time to wake up" – and in between those two frames: Absolutely nothing! Experience one: Blackout. Experience two: Waking up. This is to say: No experience whatsoever during the anesthesia, not even the experience of "nothing". The only report I can give about this is: No experience.

The only thing that happens with the body before the operation, is that this substance is put into my bloodstream and brain. Things are "peeled away" from the experience, just like when I go into deep sleep, but now, even the experiencing itself is peeled off!

Questions I had: Does experiencing require a body-mind? But the body-mind is present on the operating table… and still, no experience… How is all this related? What is it that the anesthetic does, when it seems like both the mind and the experiencing itself are interrupted? What I now, after the fact, call "not even nothing, no experiencing," is that what pure and clean consciousness is – and therefore what my real "I" is and consists of? (I admit that this question is asked in and of my limited and seemingly separate mind's perspective, and that neither the question nor possible answers would be satisfying to the mind.) A follow-up question could be: Does this anesthesia do to me something similar to what happens when my body dies?

A while later, I realize that I have complicated things. I did not "lose consciousness" during the anesthesia. Consciousness lost me. And the mind, the body, time, and space…

What was lost was what takes place in mind and thought, and in order to experience a mind and a thought, there must first be consciousness that experiences mind and thought, but consciousness needs neither mind nor thought in order to be. Of course consciousness did not disappear, because it was – and is – the prerequisite and primary for my mind to "wake up," both during anesthesia and in deep sleep. The mind can be in many states; awake, dreaming, deep sleep, anesthesia, etc – different states where things and the whole world appear differently or not at all. But consciousness has no states – all states are experienced in it.

I still have two unanswered questions that I don't have the answer to, nor do I need them answered, really, but they are interesting: How can a substance in the bloodstream and brain make it so that consciousness is no longer aware of the body-mind? And how is it that the body does not die then?

Freed mind

What we consider ourselves to have experienced thus far, is almost exclusively that our minds have been and are "imprisoned," bound to a body that we call ours.

In our eyes, it looks like that which is experiencing a body-mind is infinite because, if Consciousness would have eyes, its eyes would see so much more – yes, everything that can be seen – compared to the eyes that my mind is using. The full seeing of Consciousness is therefore not filtered through the conditioning and limitations of the localized mind. But the experience that Consciousness is having when Mischa is eating an apple is so "real" that it is possible to believe that it is reality, "his" reality. To experience the eating of an apple, pears, oranges, bananas, and everything else that isn't an apple must be excluded. This exclusion or division is an illusion, and its reality consists of Consciousness experiencing it – and everything else that is experienced right now, as all beings.

Mind, when freed from the body, can therefore only mean that there is more room then, for what is larger, more open and freer than when the mind was bound to a body.

Chasing

The chasing after becoming a better person
tells me that I don't consider myself to be
what I want to be,
or what I want to be perceived to be.

Do I believe that I could be
something other than what I am?
Or be somewhere else
than where I am?

Naturally, I am already exactly what I need to be,
and exactly where I need to be,
because I cannot be anything else,
nor can I be anywhere else.

I would be futile to even try to be that.
So the question of what and where I need to be,
or should be, falls by reason of its own absurdity.
As does the chasing.

Not true?

We perceive and express
something that is not true, every day,
e.g. when we say "darkness came,"
because "darkness" cannot be experienced.
It is the absence of light that is experienced.
"Darkness" is nothing in itself,
it does not "fall," it does not "come,"
it is just that the light is "somewhere else".
Light in itself is always the same,
and it is not changed by not being perceived.
To not perceive light is nothing,
but light is always the same.

Change?

I gave self-centeredness
and received the same,
when I had forgotten that we all consist of the same Self,
which everything originates from.

I had a desire to change
and found that no one can change,
when I had forgotten that I consist of immutability,
and that all I ever see is change.

I thought I was something
and found that it was impossible,
because I am what everything appears in,
and in myself I am nothing.

And even this very understanding…
I want to use to change things?
To try to return
to what I already am? Ha!

Ceased

When I searched high and low
and in every corner of the world,
there was no one to find,
and no one who searched,
but only the searching.
Then it ceased.

When I turned myself inside-out,
so many times and in so many different ways,
in order to find myself or something higher,
I found neither myself nor something higher,
but only the turning inside-out.
In timeless stillness, I watched it cease.

What I am

What is seen does not change that which sees.
I am not what I see, nor someone who sees.
I am seeing, and all I see, is this seeing.

What is heard does not change that which hears.
I am not what I hear, nor someone who hears.
I am hearing, and all I hear, is this hearing.

What is said does not change that which speaks.
I am not what is said, nor someone who speaks.
I am speaking, and all I say, is this speaking.

What is felt does not change that which feels.
I am not what is felt, nor someone who feels.
I am feeling, and all I feel, is this feeling.

What is experienced does not change that which experiences.
I am not what is experienced, nor someone who experiences.
I am experiencing, and all I experience, is this experiencing.

The story?

When asked who I am, my mind could start thinking and make up a story about who I am, but that would only be a story about who I am, not who I am.

The only real story about who I am is This one, right now. This is the real story about who I am. But this is better said: "This is who I am". No story is This. Who I am, is This.

Realizing that I am This, frees me from every story, stories of guilt, blame, low or high self-esteem, grandeur, pride, or stories that vindicate my reputation, and the like.

Who I am, and What I am, is Who and What I always am, in the ever spaceless and timeless Now, free from any story.

CHAPTER 3

Outward?

This chapter contains texts that originate in the small and spontaneous group that is formed, in which we love to explore being, a group that often gather at my place. We name these gatherings *Satsang* according to philosophical traditions, a word from Sanskrit where *Sat* means truth and *Sanga* means gathering. In our eagerness and joy of discovery, we write, play, sing, and dance, create a web-site and invite friends to our gatherings, we make scripts for plays, produce short films, and other things – all with an intent to spread the joy of what we have discovered. In our small community, this is sometimes regarded with not so kind eyes. Funny enough, there are even rumors that there is a new sect in town…

Proof that "you" don't exist

You cannot decide what you will do. If I were to do something completely unexpected and strange, say, lie down on the floor and start rubbing your foot, thoughts happen in you, thoughts that you cannot govern. And even if I and others tell you that I'm not dangerous or mad and that I will not hurt you, you cannot govern your thoughts, be completely relaxed, and just experience what is happening! Instead, things and thoughts happen in you that you cannot govern.

This is related to the belief that you are the one deciding everything in and around you, e.g. that you understand things better than another, that you have to defend yourself, stand up for yourself, make it so that you get what you want, etc. But it is not so! If I were to say "Stupid idiot!" to you while waving my arms around your body, things would happen in your thoughts that you cannot govern! They just happen – even if you un-derstand our present discourse! But in your perception, this is not important to you, ins-tead it is important to defend the separate individual that you think you are.

If I were to say "It is very important that you concentrate on what I am saying now, and that you don't think about anything else" – you cannot do it! You cannot even do what I am asking you to do, no matter how much you want to do it. Thoughts may come, about the weather, or that I slur my speech, or whatever else.

You cannot do what you want, either. Actually, you cannot do anything! What you think is you, is more like a small, dry leaf in the wind. You think you can, you think that you are separate, that you can run things, you think you have to defend and assert, and a lot of other things. But it is not so – things just happen!

But, parallel to everything happening around what you think is you – the you that we have concluded cannot do anything or run things – another thing happens: You understand what I'm saying! These things happen simultaneously. What you think is you cannot do anything, since there is no separate you! There is a lot of thoughts, emotions, perceptions, sensations, and events that you cannot govern, because they just happen. Yet there is an understanding of what I'm saying, every detail of it. There is something that perceives everything, understands everything, hears, sees, and feels everything. There is something that really is completely reliable in this regard, something that always stays the same, that simply is, understands, hears, sees, feels and is wide open for what is, that loves everything, and accepts everything. It is – simultaneously with the thought, belief, or idea that there is a separate "you" in there that can decide for itself that he will do this or that now, think this or that now – but that is not you! Even the idea of a separate "you" is also something that happens!

The only existence, is that which understands what I'm saying. And it… is the same. The same, everywhere, and always. It is I, and you, and we, and everyone, and every-thing. There is only being. It is very reliable. Be it!

Consumed

Remember once when you were completely consumed, dissolved, enraptured, when "time stood still".

Remember what was happening around you. Was it really what happened around you that did something to you? Probably not, because there have been others in the same situation who did not feel what you did. Probably not, because you might have been in exactly the same situation before, without it feeling the way it did later.

Was it you who did something to yourself? Probably not, because you may have done similar things before, but not felt that way.

What remains, is that things happen, and that you are that which experiences them.

Test!

Close your eyes. Listen to a sound.
Where does the hearing happen? Inside you?
Probably, no obviously, in consciousness.

Open your eyes. Where is the world seen?
Also in you, or rather, and obviously, in consciousness.

Impersonal

Consciousness is intimate, but not personal or individual.
All properties of consciousness are in the same way impersonal and non-individual.

The mystery

The mystery is not how we can be one with everything and each other
as the same consciousness.

The mystery is how we – who **are** one with everything in the same consciousness –
in our thinking have been able to divide the world into objects and subjects
that are separate from each other.

The story

When we first met, I said "you" to you,
that I like to be with you,
hear you, and to see you.
I know what this "you" is,
the "you" that is reading these words right now,
but I posit that you don't know what this "you" is.

What you think "you" are, is actually a story.
You think you are the baby that was born,
the kid who learned how to walk,
who went to a school where you got grades,
the young one who got that first job,
fell in love with someone and started a family.

What I will tell you now
does not disrespect or negate any of that,
nor any of the joys or sorrows that you have felt.
All of that is a story, though,
but what you are, is what is seeing that story,
just as I am seeing that story.

You see that story from a first person perspective,
and I see that story from a second person perspective.
But here's the kicker:
It is the same story.
And you are that which is seeing that story.
And so am I.

So if you and I are seeing that story,
neither you nor I are that story.
First or second person perspective,
doesn't make the story you, nor me.
So what you and I are is the same,
observing that story.

Whatever we observe, touch, hear, or feel,
is not what we essentially are.
We are that which is experiencing all that.
You say that you see me,
and I say that I see you.
And that which sees me, is what sees you.

What you call "you" is something we experience,
and not what either of us are.
The "me" that you say I am, is also something we both experience,
not what either of us are.
So since you and I experience both "you" and "me,"
we are neither. We are what is experiencing both. The same.

It is what you call "you" and "me" that are different,
but they are actually only stories,
experienced by what we both are,
which is this selfsame "I" that experiences.
This selfsame "I" contains both "you" and "me" –
and the whole world.

What I have proposed here, is one way of looking at it.
Another way of looking at it, is that
when I say that I see you, and you say that you see me,
it is actually this selfsame "I" that sees itself.
What we are seeing happens in what we now know is the same,
that this selfsame "I" appears as both "you" and "me".

When we see and feel Reality in this way of looking at it,
we see beneath what we could call "the surface of things,"
and we see the Reality of the appearances of "you" and "me".
A consequence of seeing each other this way,
and the whole world for that matter,
is that I see you as myself, as well as my neighbor, and the whole world.

Whatever I do to you, and to the whole world,
I am doing to myself, since we all are this selfsame Self.

You only see yourself

You hate your neighbor who has the nice car and the nice house. But he always does something wrong. Maybe things don't always go wrong, but you think that he always does something wrong. You go about nagging and scolding him, accusing him for things he has or hasn't done, but you feel that he should be scolded.

The neighbor, on the other hand, understands. When you scold him, he just stands there calmly and loves you, because he knows that your words say nothing about him. It is as though he's from another world. And in a way, he is. And on this level, you never meet.

I got news: You see only yourself. You want do believe that you are a good person who chooses to do good things, takes good care of his car and his house, and behaves in a good way. But you hate yourself so deeply, because you have never been free from judgment, hatred, and the scolding from others, never in your whole life. Be it your dad, grandma, teacher, class-mates or partners who scolded, doesn't matter. You still live with and in that self-image. And since you only see yourself, the neighbor is an idiot, whatever he does!

So what about the neighbor, then, who lives in the understanding that he is everything, one with everything, and that everything is one with him, in and as the same Consciousness? He, too, sees only himself. He sees you with love and tolerance, and is neither angry nor enraged with you.

You see only yourself.

Love your neighbor – as yourself.

Remember

Always remember:
Whatever changes your experience –
alcohol, medical drugs, or psychoactive drugs,
depression or euphoria,
disgust or love –
no content of Consciousness alters Consciousness.
Everything is in and of this one and selfsame Consciousness.
This one and selfsame consciousness is You.

Promise

You can get better at doing things
in this illusory and always changing world.
You can exercise the body so that it works better.
You can exercise the intellect so that it thinks better.
You can even exercise your emotional life,
so that you become better at feeling,
and better at understanding the feelings of others.
But that which experiences all this,
you can do nothing about.
Not in the physical, intellectual, or emotional, anyway.
The only thing you can do
is to forget what it is that experiences
and live your life as though it did not exist,
as if what you are lives in your body,
or in your thoughts, or somewhere else.

But I promise you:
If you find out what you are,
so that you understand what you really are –
the unchanging
that experiences all this,
and that everything actually lives in what you are –
then you may still exercise the body so that it works better,
exercise the intellect so that it thinks better,
and exercise your emotional life so that you become better at feeling.
But before, it was so important
because you identified with it,
and you thought you had to become better at it,
in order to "become somebody," or become a "better person".
When you know what you are,
this is surely not as important any longer.
At least it is not something to identify with.
And like so many before you,
you will surely say:
– Wow, everything happens by itself!

One reality

There exists only one reality.
You are it.

But "one reality" is saying too much.
Because then there could be more.
All we can say
about the only reality is:
It is not two.

Shout!

Just as the road to here – a world of lust for power and money in separation – was taken
by a multitude of people who had forgotten that they are one in love, the road to there –
a world of love, one in Being – can be taken by a multitude of people who remember
that they are one in love. So, my dear: Remember! When you have remembered, shout
it from the rooftops!

Humiliated?

Only the ego, which does not have a separate existence, can be humiliated.

Be

To just be
is a wonderful experience!
But completely independent
of illusory gain or loss,
from the perspective of the ego.
When you are sad – only be.
When you are glad – only be.
Only be.

Ego wins?

Consciousness does not have an issue with an ego appearing.
This is why the ego always "wins".

Reversed

You have a mind, and everything else.
You lack nothing.

You are not a mind that lacks something,
even if the mind always lacks something.

Mind will never understand You,
because it is in You.

You understand the mind,
because it is in You.

Back

If you remember
where you came from – awareness –
you can never loose your place if you go back.
Because you are always that.

And going back is always here,
because we are talking about it,
while we are remembering
where we came from.

Let's go back!
And find ourselves
right where we are.
All is well.

Change

The Unchangeable
sees only change.

Mine?

It is not my intelligence.
It is intelligence.
It is not my riches.
It is riches.
Everything is one,
expressing itself as difference forms.
Nothing is "mine".

What happens when "mine" is let go of?
Infinite intelligence?
Infinite love, riches?

When "mine" is added, everything is divided,
diminished, seen to be personal.
That's when time, energy, and money is invested
in making a better "me," more intelligent, famous, rich…

It cannot be "my" richness,
because this "me" has no separate existence.
But even if we don't agree with this,
the idea can be very attractive – communism, socialism…
To share everything is for most of us an attractive utopia,
but it whispers clearly of its origin of no separation.

If a human does not hold onto "his" intelligence or riches,
in a culture where it is enforced to do so,
it almost always happens that he is consumed, exploited, or silenced,
as in the case of many, the likes of Ghandi, Jesus…
A small group absorbs, suffocates, and silences
this expression of the collective.

The collective letting go of "me,"
letting go of the identification with the body,
the realization that we are one,
is the ultimate expression of love.

Alienated?

To begin with, it might sound alienated, cold, and emotionless, to realize what I am…

…that I am not the person that I think I am, that I don't have to be in a certain conditioned way, don't have to behave in a certain conditioned way, don't need a certain education, that I don't have to build on my own or others' stories about how to make a good future, in order to become something worthwhile in the world. To no longer believe that, and to let go of all identification with the illusory person that I thought I was, and to let go of all false ideas about what I could be.

Does this sound like I would alienate myself from reality, that I no longer care about what happens in the world? If I sit with this for a while, I will soon realize that it's actually the other way around!

When I have let go of all the ideas about what I thought I was, when I no longer strive to become what I or others thought I should be in the world – what remains is only what I am, namely what sees and experiences everything. Like right now, when I'm reading this, without thinking about anything else!

I see everything that happens. I don't meddle with what is happening based on my own or others' preconceived ideas, but I only see things for what they are.

And all of a sudden, the seeing becomes a doing. Like when the stroller is on its way to roll out into the street in front of a speeding truck. I see it and run to protect the child from getting hurt.

If, instead, I would act from false ideas about whether it is worthwhile to save the child or not, or stop and calculate if I will have time to run to prevent an accident – then I miss out on being involved in what is happening. If I act based on these ideas, things will not work out well.

We know already that most of man's biggest activities on the planet are not working out well – we who have tried to be so smart, intelligent, well educated, scientific… well, this is how it turned out!

If I, instead, just am what I am, and only see… I will do things that resonate with the understanding of what I am, and act accordingly. Suddenly, I see what needs to be done – if a person is in danger, I try prevent it, if someone is bleeding, I bandage the wounds, if someone is crying, I cry with him, and become the comfort I would need if I felt their sorrow, I become the friend and security for the one who believes that security is to be found somewhere else than in himself. I see, and I do.

Already, I hear how intimate and close it becomes! How it actually becomes limitless, both what I see and what I do. Because I act without false ideas. And simply am.

Missing understanding

There is an understanding that is often missing. It becomes evident as soon as we speak about whether it is Consciousness or mind that experiences, if I can govern my thoughts or not, if there is free will, etc.

The understanding is that what we are talking about – and have varying opinions about, and the fact that we are even talking, and hearing, listening, talking, and thinking, not to mention the writing and reading of this text – is how Consciousness experiences itself, is what it looks like, right now!

You consist of Consciousness that experiences, no more or less, but solely! And always! And everywhere, since You are everything. Just like I am!

Robots cannot become conscious

You can get a machine to perform very complex tasks, ordinarily attributed to only human capacity. But you cannot get a machine to have the experience of performing those tasks, much less to have the experience of being – which is so ordinary and intimate to the human experience. We are not our brains, and even though machines may perform similarly to our brains, machines will never be anything else than creations of our minds. As such, they will never get or develop Consciousness. No thing has ever gotten or developed Consciousness, but all things, all matter, including our brains and machines, appear in Consciousness.

Machines cannot understand, because they are made by mind and in mind. That which understands, stands under mind and certainly machines. That which stands under, stands prior to everything that manifests by, of, and as itself.

Ordered

The brain is subordinate to the mind, which perceives what is practical for the organism, when objects, black and white, contrasts, discrimination is needed by it.

The mind is subordinate to Consciousness, which experiences itself through it, i.e. what is manifested in, out of, and as itself.

When it is believed in the mind that mind is superior, highest, ideas are formed, ideas that are far beyond "what is practical" for the organism, things that are not in unison with the above.

But none of what everything Is and consists of – Consciousness – is affected by, or affects anything that is not in unison with it, because it is what everything is and consists of, and contains everything.

With knowing

What is called "humans" are not conscious. The seemingly separate human understands nothing in itself, but possesses only knowledge. Consciousness is what understands seemingly separate "humans".

Only Consciousness understands anything at all. Understanding cannot be communicated (between seemingly two), but can only be experienced, because understanding is what "we" always are and consist of, the very Knowing in consciousness (Latin: "with knowing"). This Knowing is all knowing – all that can be known is known by the same Knowing – which therefore only experiences the Knowing about itSelf. Knowledge (Greek *gnosis*), on the other hand, can be communicated (between seemingly two), and is therefore not Knowing in the prior sense, and is not what we consist of.

That which Knows, is what we always are. What we consist of, is never more or less conscious, even though the seemingly separate human can forget it. **And** remember it!

This is I!

It is the same Consciousness that has eight billion human experiences, and many more seagull-experiences, yet more fly-experiences, in the infinity of Consciousness!

It is the same Consciousness that experiences a Mischa that writes this text now, and the same Consciousness that experiences a you that reads it. The experience that you can claim is separate from Mischa's experience is the same experience, the same Consciousness experiencing all this, in itSelf, in an infinitely multi-colored and multi-sounding cavalcade of… experiencing!

How can I be sure of this? Well, we who are experienced in the same Consciousness can talk about the same things, the same color of the sky, or the same taste of an apple, we can talk about this, being precisely what is experienced right now (e.g. that Mischa is sitting here writing this, and that you "on the other side of the paper" is reading this). We completely agree on this, because we are the same Consciousness that experiences it! We also agree that someone may not agree with this, and thinks that this is utter madness – well, then that is also what is experienced, by the same Consciousness, in Consciousness' one and the same experience!

So, stand up, lift your hands and say:

–"I am I, it is I who is I, and I am all this, and I love my Self! And I love You and You and You… I love everyone here, and all this! Because You and everything is in Me. And not only that – You are I, I am You, and You are Me."

If this is not loving your neighbor as yourself, I don't know what is! This is I, loving my Self, through all and everything!

Namaste!

Light

I am light.
Not an individual light source,
but the light itself!
I am the light that makes it possible
to see anything at all,
as well as individual light sources.

No answers

There are no answers here,
so don't look for answers in what is said.
Only hear what is said.
The answer is on your end.

Circular reasoning

If you think that what you think
is important, it will feel like it is,
and that it is so, that it is important.

It is then possible to interpret that feeling
as evidence for it being really important.

Such outstanding circular reasoning!

Prior to expression

No expression of love is love.
No expression of truth is truth.

Love and truth are
prior to every expression,
and the reality of every expression.

See how obvious this becomes:
All that mankind really wants, is love.
"Everything that is possible to believe,
is an image of truth."

What is before every expression?
Whatever we are,
see that we are before the expressions.
See that we are love and truth.

Our boundaries

If love is boundless, which everyone
who is completely absorbed by it
experiences –
then it is obvious that all our our defenses
and protection mechanisms
is the boundary that
we ourselves set for love –
which apparently is so boundless
that it also gives space for
our setting of boundaries.

I Corinthians 13:7–8
[It] beareth all things,
believeth all things,
hopeth all things,
endureth all things.
Charity never faileth.

What is searching?

Are you looking for your True self?

Stop looking, and only be…
what is looking!

This is what you – and I – Are!

See

The world is not how you think,
it is how you see.

End?

You are what appears as all forms,
and that which experiences this appearance.
Confusing form with what you are,
creates suffering.

Is the world coming to an end?
Some people think so.
But you are here, experiencing this,
and so is "everyone else".
Since no one has reported of
an end of experiencing,
nor a beginning of it,
you are safe.

Because you are this,
so is "everyone else".
This is how welcome you are,
in this reality,
because there is no other.
Drop the idea of "other"
and just be this.

Perspectives

Actually, no perspective
is based on reality.
All perspectives consist of
the same infinite field of view of consciousness,
because there is no reference point
in what seeing occurs in.

All attempts to find a perspective
create conceptual separation.
If we look closer at this separation,
it shows itself to be just what it is:
Nothing.

My (long) love-letter to mySelf

Mind-altering substances? Yes. Coffee, sugar, alcohol…
Food? Yes, mind full of "hungry" turns into mind full of "satiated".
Music? Yes. Movies? Yes. Books? Yes. Confrontations? Yes.
Every thing is mind-altering?
And mind is altering all things?
Yes, in a sense.
The state of mind constantly changes.
As does the state of things,
which depends on projections of the mind.
There is no good state of mind,
nor a bad state of mind.
No good state of things,
nor bad state of things.
Just state of mind.
And state of things.

"On this side of" all changes of mind, there is the unchanging.
All changes occur in what is unchanging.
That which experiences mind, is always the same –
or we could not talk about the changes.
That which experiences the changes (and everything else)
is never changing, always at rest, allowing everything,
open to whatever happens,
does not interfere, nor control*,
just loving whatever flows within itself.
Is it not the case,
that whenever something has happened,
the real You just saw it happen?
And that nothing has affected the real You?
You are still that which has experienced all of it,
and You are here to tell the story.
Is that not You, the real You?
What else would it be?
Who else would it be?

Would You say that You controlled any of it?
Or did it just happen?
Knowing what the real You is,
do You feel a need to control
whatever flows within You?
Are You not so intimately one
with what flows in You,
that none of what happens,
really matters?
Is not all of it really You?
And seeing that,
is not everything okey?

Are You not, in fact,
overtaken by everything that happens,
so one with it,
that there is no difference,
no separation,
between You and what happens?
Where would the line be drawn?
Where would the boundary be?
Is there anything You can do
to change what is happening,
or is it just happening?
Trying to change it,
would also just be what is happening…

To let go,
to just let whatever happens happen,
is that not equanimity?
Total peace and rest,
allowing, seeing everything happen.
Flowing with it,
flowing in You.
Is that not the Holiest of Holies?
Just being what happens.

Does it move You?
Or are You the movement?
Can You distinguish anything
from anything else,
or is everything just moving,
all as one movement,
in a never changing You?

If everything that happens
is familiar and like home to You,
what could disturb that peace?
You are the silence, in which all hearing takes place,
the void where everything forms,
the light that makes everything visible.

All this is My creating, My creation,
and never would I give it
the power to separate itself from Me,
as I am both the Creator and the Created,
and all I see is mySelf,
playing out what only looks like
it is independent of Me.
All the earthly years of My experience of being You,
and the experiences themselves,
is simply Myself.

I cannot make this more obvious to You,
and all mankind's explanations
about what all this really is,
always fall short.
It is so obvious,
it is not even right in front of You,
it is in You,
right where You are –
in Me.

Do You think that You can put Your hand to what is happening?
That You somehow could alter
what is I, the Creator and the Created?
Can the river of events
steer itself?
How arrogant to even think so!
Everything that happens,
including that You may want to change something,
is My, and only My creating,
and in Me, there are no high horses to sit on!
You are the stream in My hand,
and I steer it wherever I want.
You are created only to run and flow freely,
and not for fighting or resisting,
although this, too, is entirely up to You.

Just flow!
Be thankful for the grace to be able to do that.
And just enjoy the ever changing landscape of life,
which can never prevent You from always returning
to mySelf, the infinite Ocean.
You can be completely safe,
it is I who create and Am all this,
and I don't let anything go to waste,
because I love My whole creation,
and everything in it,
because I am it.
You can see this,
from a distance, so to speak,
and feel My eternal heartbeats in You,
because I am You.
You can enter the creation,
and play Your part,
in gratitude and reverence for Me,
because You see Me be everything.

You are My love!
Be it, and anything can happen,
but never forget Me, never leave My side,
for then it may look like I have abandoned You.
And remember that I am very jealous
if it still were to happen,
and that I will never give up
My search for You!
Be calm!
It would take a lot for a mother
to abandon her own child,
but for Me it is impossible,
because I really am You.
Wherever I see, I see only mySelf,
so let Yourself expand
beyond all the unsurmountable limitations of mind,
so that You see,
that I am You.

Then, You see Me always and everywhere.
Nothing is anything else
than forms in, from, and by Me,
and You fall down mute, in humility,
in awe of My greatness,
that is You, simultaneously.
Your gratitude has no end,
for partaking
so intimately with Me
in My creating,
now and always,
without end.
Or beginning.
Is Your limited mind reeling now?
Good, let it reel! Breathe out.
No mind is made to encompass this,
but only to be My Creation, as it is,
and I have created Your mind to only serve You.
Not the other way around.

Be overwhelmed, raptured, euphoric,
before the greatness of Me being You.
Or be sad or disappointed over something
that takes place in Me.
But see that I take care of My Creation,
and that that I never ever abandon You.
You are forever My beloved,
and forever, simultaneously,
without delay or waiting,
always mySelf,
without distance or boundary.
In this way You can feel and see
that we are one,
You, My Creation and I.
You see it!
You are it!

I am tireless in My creating,
and there's room for everything –
even for Your doubting it!
But don't doubt,
for then it may look like You
have deficiencies and shortcomings,
that You would not be enough,
that You somehow should be blamed
for what has happened or not.
Oh, such misunderstanding!
Now, see YourSelf for what You Are –
Me in creating.
Does it seem too grand
and completely intangible?
It is!
For it is My nature, not Yours.
You are an image of Me,
just like everything else.
Not the other way around.

Maybe, when You remember this –
as before Your body was born into the world –
You will finally have peace, My Beloved.
We are really not two.
Welcome home!
To where You have always been,
where You have never left.

P.S.
Do You know "how many" Me are necessary
to create a world?
This many, just as many as there are!
And not only eight billion humans,
oh no!
My infiniteness is reflected
in the whole universe,
from mankind's constant search
for his Self, which is I,
through all beings and things,
innumerable,
to the outermost and innermost invisible.
"Where wast thou when I laid the foundations of the earth?"

❦

Moses and the Preacher

The Bible is life-threatening! At least for our imagined earthly life:

Genesis 3:19
In the sweat of thy face
shalt thou eat bread,
till thou return unto the ground;
for out of it wast thou taken:
for dust thou art,
and unto dust shalt thou return.

Ecclesiastes 12:7
Then shall the dust return to the earth as it was:
and the spirit shall return unto God who gave it.

If you really go all the way with this,
that you are separate from everything else,
and your very own Lord,
who must protect his own,
in the struggle for survival of matter,
then hear what your destiny is:
You are dust.
Returning to the same dust.

You are soil, living on soil.
You are, live and move
in and of the same dust you come from,
without ever leaving this perfect cycle.
If you see only soil,
you are only soil,
which you have imagined
to be your nature and destiny.

As soil, you move soil,
feed on it, yourself,
make your brand from the same soil
that you shall return as.
And in no way
do you change anything,
but you only play a while
in the mud of impermanence.

But hear what you have forgotten,
listen to what has been said:
What you have always known,
and always experienced
all the movements of the world in – is spirit.
The same spirit
that you are given from and of,
that you as dust have only imagined
to be a God, as separate from everything as yourself.

Human, you are but a vessel,
filled up with what sees itself,
spirit that sees itself animated.
The earth and all its movements,
is not, and has never been you,
but only what you have experienced,
you who are spirit,
returning to the same spirit.

The same spirit that gives of and from itSelf,
and always remains its true Self,
independently of how the earth moves,
in what spirit experiences itSelf in.
Let soil be soil,
and be what you really are:
Spirit living in spirit, never leaving its home.

You recognize, re-discover,
what you have felt deep inside,
through everything you have experienced,
the statutory dance of matter –
that it consists of what it appears in,
the very superior, highest,
which without any effort
keeps the universe safely in its bosom.

Hear how spirit calls you by name,
calls out to you that you may hear,
that you are the same spirit,
that always returns to,
and comes from
itSelf.
Don't be worried, my beloved
for we are the same infinite and eternal.

Understand and feel how you can relax,
and see the dance of matter for what it is,
while you remain what you always are:
That which everything experienced
has its life, its movements, in, of, and from.
It is never afraid of itSelf,
but it always welcomes
every vibration in itSelf.

Now is time to celebrate, now is time to dance,
in the re-discovery of your Self.
Let everything happen the way it always has,
in your Self, the reality of everything.
Your shackles have never fettered you,
so now you can fully enjoy your journey,
from the constant movements of the earth
back to your Self!

Your neighbor

It seems hard to understand the sentence
"Love your neighbor as yourself".
Most often, something is added to it, which changes its meaning, like this:
"Love your neighbor as **_you love_** yourself"

The sentence is actually similar to these, and they are not hard to understand:
Regard your neighbor as yourself.
See your neighbor as yourself.
Treat your neighbor as yourself.

The sentence really means this:
You are your neighbor.
Love your neighbor, who you are.
Your neighbor is nothing else than yourself, you.

See

Seeing and what is seen
are not two.

This seeing neither hinders,
nor affects, nor is affected by
anything that is seen.

Calm

Play with the thought
(because that's all it is,
occurring in, by, and consisting of You):
Could God create something
that would scare Him?
Outrageous, right?

Take that thought home, one step closer.
The thought occurred in,
and consisted of You.
Bring it home to You.
Become the thought –
which you already are.
Ask Yourself, out of which
everything is made:
Could something occur in, by,
and consist of You,
that would scare You?

Fear is only a belief,
also occurring in, by,
and consisting of You.
A belief that somehow –
contrary to all evidence and reason,
and all experience ever investigated –
there could be a separate "you"
that does **not** occur in,
and does **not** consist of
Your imperturbable Self.

So there is only peace,
in being what we all are,
my brother, sister, mother, father.
I can see no beginning, nor end,
of what we have always been.
If there is cause for celebration,
forever dancing in awe of creation,
this is it – our Self-induced world.

You are the world

You are okey.
You are exactly where
every atom in the Universe
is supposed to be, right now.

There may still be the belief that
"this is true of the Universe,
but not of me" –
a very common feeling.

But you are not of this world.
You are on the right track.
You don't know how right you are.
You are not a product of this world.

Others may ask:
What about the world, then?
You can then lovingly tell them
that the world is in you.

Because the world is in you,
there's nothing to worry about.
All is well.
Breathe, listen. Partake or don't.
Just realize and be
what you now know you are.

If circumstances are simple or difficult,
this realization is the easiest of them all,
it is absolutely effortless.
It is always the other way around,
from what the world told you.

You are not a human
having a spiritual experience,
You are Spirit
having a human experience.

Is this a question of semantics?
No, it is a matter of national emergency –
no, global emergency!
Not about fear of what might happen
to individuals fighting for survival –
I am here to tell you
that there's nothing to worry about –
because the world is in you.
Think about that for a while.

Whatever happens to the world
does not affect what you are.
That is what all of this actually means.

You can verify this for yourself.
Take a common human
expression of hope:
"I hope things will be better tomorrow".
No one has ever experienced a future,
and experience is the test of reality.
Any experience is always real.
And that which experiences them,
is never afraid.

You are the background
on which the world is painted.
So, yes, you can say:
"I am the world."

Do you want to talk about
all the forms in Consciousness?
Or do you want to not only talk about,
but also knowingly be Consciousness?
The selfsame Consciousness,
that encompasses
every expression
in and of itself.

Open yourself to the possibility
that what I am saying can be true.
Then, see what happens.

You are this

My beloved.
Stop searching.
Listen to me, for just a little while.
Let me tell you,
wherever you are:
How could you ever look out
on whatever you call the world,
except from where you are?
Whatever you find,
is only your Self.

Whatever your perception is,
it is laden with filters
and limitations of the mind.
What are you, I ask,
without those filters and limitations?
Set them aside,
put them on the shelf for a while –
which we do, anyway,
every night we go into deep sleep.
You don't have to think, feel,
or do anything.

When you are totally relaxed,
everything is fine.
What I am talking **about**,
is what I am talking **to**,
and where I am talking **from**.
It is your home.

You are this.
See how it is so much?
So rich, with colors, depth,
emotions, tastes, fragrances,
planets, solar systems everywhere.
It is so vast.
You are all this.

This is the "more" you have always
wanted to experience.
This, right here, is the "more"
you always wanted to be.
You always knew
that you could be something more,
and you strived for it,
through educations, professions,
relationships, possessions, and more.

I am here to tell you:
You are already that!
You are the "more"
you always wanted out of life.
Because, remember:
Anything you find,
anything that is true,
anything that is not true,
you find right where you are.
You can never be anywhere else
than where you are.
That is also, of course,
where you understand
that from out of your Self,
ten thousand things
are created.

Just be that.
End of story.
When you see this,
you know that you are the Silence,
in which every sound,
and every manifestation
of your Self
is born.

Disappointment?

Expectations always happen.
Disappointment has only to do with
how much "attachment" there is to them,
in the belief that their fulfillment or not
affects what I am.

In everything!

It is not nature
that expresses itself in mathematics,
it is nature that expresses itself
in that someone sees it.
So see it in everything!

It is not love
that expresses itself in the new infatuation,
it is love that expresses itself
in that someone feels it.
So feel it in everything!

It is not happiness that expresses itself
in the new career,
it is happiness that expresses itself
in that someone thinks so.
So have it in everything!

It is not peace that expresses itself
in peace movements,
it is peace that expresses itself
in that someone acts peacefully.
So act it in everything!

Love the children

Loving your own children regardless of
everything you may call good or bad
about them or their life, actually comes
from the intimate understanding that love
and acceptance has nothing to do with
history.

Why would this understanding
not be applicable to every being?

The apparent difference between belief systems and experiencing reality as it is

In a religion, when I believe that I have found or reached "the highest," it is still "outside me" and not "I," and it also feels that way. What I have found then, is "outside me," and I can never be certain that it is what it seems to be, or what it is claimed to be.

The "religion" of materialism is the same way. Look at an atom, see what it consists of, conclude that it is electrons and other things, look at what they consist of, come to the end of that and see that it is actually empty, or made up of strings of possibilities. It is outside me, not I, and therefore uncertain.

If I believe that I have reached the highest, it is still not "I". Thus, in belief systems, there is the possibility of doubt. Doubt is the distance between what I know that I am, and what I believe I have reached or should reach. The best I can have in my faith, is that my conviction is strong, and that my faith is unshakeable.

It is really the same with all ideas about something that I think is outside myself. Communism, scientology, pantheism, and all other -isms. We already know most everything about the psychological mechanisms of belief systems.

When representatives of two different belief systems argue, it is never possible for anyone to "win," because the ones who argue already know deeply that the foundation of a belief system – that I and everything else is separate – is something that does not match reality. Basing things on a foundation that doesn't match reality, everything becomes "skewed" somehow – because nothing in reality is separate.

In the ultimate, highest, in religions or any other belief system, there is a built-in skewness that we already intuitively feel, since they are based on ideas that are 180° from reality, e.g. that "matter is the origin of consciousness" (where even the concept of "origin" is skewed). Thus, the argumentation becomes laborious and complicated, and this shows in many ways in various contexts, and the horizon for what is possible to find out, teasingly moves further away.

But – to experience reality as it is, is therefore not a belief, but an experienced fact: Everything that is experienced, is experienced by what I am, no matter what that is. This is also very easy to verify, prior to when the filters of the mind are applied and thoughts begin.

In the experience of reality as it is, there is neither any distance between that which experiences it and what is experienced. That, in turn, naturally means that the identification with the body – previously believed to be separate – ceases. When the body is experienced for what it is, namely just the same as "everything else," i.e. matter – concepts grounded in separation cease, concepts that limited the mind to opinions about time, space, distance, matter, causality, etc.

When I see reality for what it is, I also see what I am. I see that there is no difference between what I am and what "something else" is. And then I don't need to say that I believe in something. The closest, most true that I can say, is that I experience that I am.

Neither can I say that how I see is another way to see reality – because it only is, and is always what it is. It is not a "type of experience," since there are no "types of experiences" – there is only this experience of what is, including all forms that appear in what is, even the talk about different types of experiences! The forms include all billions of people and innumerable other beings and things.

Like Ibn Arabi said (sort of):
Consciousness sleeps in the rocks.
Consciousness dreams in the plants.
Consciousness moves in the animals.
Consciousness wakes up in man, and sees itself.

And that is what is happening now. We see ourselves and that we consist of the same Consciousness, that is and experiences everything.

Only Consciousness

There is only Consciousness.
Not one. Not more.
Consciousness of all this,
of all of this Universe,
in this Consciousness.
So, naturally, we will find no other.
Consciousness being conscious,
not only as and through the minds of us humans,
but of everything possible to be conscious of,
as and through every mind.
That same consciousness,
perfect, whole, and complete as it is,
neither wants, needs nor desires any other,
because it is what contains
every want, need, and desire.

Talking to myself

It is the sound of silence that allows for every tone.
It is the emptiness that holds every space.
It is out of absolute emptiness,
every thing and activity is manifest.

There is only this,
and it can look like you are seeing it well,
by realizing what you are,
and that everything takes place in you.

What I am talking about, is all happening in what I am,
including every perspective.
Every perspective held, is an echo from the field of possibilities,
which in, by and out of itself forms itself as worlds,
effortlessly and beyond any attempt to produce them.

What we are left with, all we can say about "all this,"
is that we undoubtably are whatever it is that is understanding
these words, and that "this" and everything else
is what is going on in what I am.

It is therefore not "one's perspective,"
but every "one's perspective" that is going on.
Or rather "no perspective,"
because every perspective
of good and bad, black and white…
all balance each other out "in the end".
And we are also that "end".

Does this realization hurt us? No.
It only removes any possibility of diminishing yourself
to "your own view" of yourself, to where you can feel like
a puny little separate being that is the victim
of what every one else thinks of you.

Every constellation of opinions about "you"
is a reflection of all efforts, all endeavors,
all seeking, all desires,
of all humanity of all times.
If you want to reduce yourself to that, that is also okay –
because you know who I am talking to,
you know that you are that which knows
that all this is so. That's it!

Trying to explain this, would only produce wind,
because we cannot describe what is, but only what it looks like.

Realizing this, makes living very easy, rational, and simple.
What your organism needs to sustain itself,
including everything that happens to it – hunger, thirst, ups and downs –
is just what happens in what you are.
And all that is okay, as you do not need any identification
with any of it.

For the able – who dares!

Listen to the most wonderful music you know,
the piece that evokes the sweetest, deepest emotions in you.
Listen and take note when it feels the strongest.
When you feel the depth, let yourself be embraced by it and stay there.

Is the experience not true?
Is the experience not there, when the music and you meet?
Can you experience how the music and you are one in this experience?
Or the other way around:
Can you experience any border between the music and the experience?
Can one be without the other?

Now, can you also leave behind all your memories of and stories surrounding the music?
Can you feel the naked, the raw, the completely engrossing?
Can you feel that beyond all stories, it is as if what always is there,
is both where and what you are now?
Can you see it as if where you are now, is like a room that is always there,
and that it has no door?
Does it even feel like you went into a room? Is it even a room?

Can you be open, just like when you were engrossed,
open to the possibility that you really always are there?
And that you only "forgot" it, when you were entangled in the mundane?
The mundane that seems to always change, seems to never be the same?

When engrossed, the experience is always the same.
You are the same, even when the music changes, or even stops.
When engrossed, you probably have neither age nor gender.
You and the experience are one.

Precisely there, it can feel like everything you thought you were
dissolves, disappears, dies…
As if you are jumping out, fall into an unknown space filled with love.
Yet, it is so true, so experiential, so real!

But know! Know that in this unshakable certainty,
you are what is experiencing everything, and everything you experience!
The border between what you experience and what is experiencing just isn't there!
When you are there, to claim:
–"I am separate from everything else" becomes alien and unreal.

Informed by this unshakable certainty, what happens when you "go out into the world"?
Is there any essential difference between what you are when engrossed in music
and what you are in the world?
When you no longer see any difference, what happens then?
One thing is certain:
What happens then, or ever, neither removes nor adds anything
to what you already are.

It is always 180° from what we've been taught

I can never look for reality,
because I already and always am it.
I can never come to a better future,
because I already and always am what comes.
I can never return to something better,
because I already and always am what returns.
I can never go outside the body to be somewhere else,
because the body and all other places already and always are in me.
I can never fight for peace,
because I already and always am peace.
I can never be afraid to die,
because I am not born.

Dangerous?

There is nothing inherently dangerous.
What is dangerous, is believing that something is,
and then acting on that belief.

Our direct experience of what we inherently Are,
is unfathomable peace.
Acting on this, is definitely not dangerous.

This is how it is

Either you just buy into it and play along,
buy new trainers or a new car when they should be bought.
Sometimes you win, sometimes you lose,
in the competition with your colleagues.
At home you sometimes win, but most of the time you lose,
when the partner wins your fights, being so smart,
and you just feel like a fool, ridiculous.
This mismatch always leaves room for an agenda
that is all about power-play.
Have fun with that!

Or…
step out of all your roles!
What remains?
Can you understand and feel that you are the actor?
Or have you played all your roles so well, so fervently,
that you have forgotten what you Are?

Dissociated?

If we make a difference between what is experiencing
and what is experienced,
we are already frighteningly close
to feeling dissociated.

When someone who is in this situation comes into contact with non-dualism
according to the usual path of "Neti, Neti" ("I am not, I am not"),
after this someone have lived their whole life in dissociation,
this path is excellent for taking the last step,
to completely freak out – as mind,
because this someone believes that one is one's mind.

The mind can acquire for itself
nice labels, like spiritual and enlightened,
while nothing has really happened with it,
other than having embraced something nice
that was said thousands of years ago, or now by me…

…while what it's really all about
is to be precisely this:
That which is experienced,
from these lines of text
to that which understands these words, as they are the same.
So, don't search for something outside of yourself
in order to understand what you are.
To understand this, you sometimes have to
stop searching altogether,
shut your eyes and be quiet.

When you have shut your eyes and are quiet,
and thoughts stop by themselves…
If this isn't the only way
to find out what you already are,
then I don't know.

My Self

It is so magnificent to be all this!
When I am music in your ears,
and you realize that you are One with Me,
you know that You and I
are one and the same,
birthing the World as it appears,
to experience MySelf,
being all this!

3D-world?

No, this is not a 3D-world,
it is the experience of a 3D-world.
My experiencing it, creates it.
But don't think about that,
as that would only be
the experience of thinking.
And don't mistake yourself
for the 3D-world,
but I admit; it would be easy.
Let's be that which experiences
this 3D-world. Peace, bro!
It's nice to know what you are.
We are the World!

Cross-eyed

Cross your eyes
while looking at a candle
burning with a still flame.
Watch how what you know
is one flame becomes two.
See the illusion.
See how the "two" are identical,
and yet the same.
But always
really
indivisible.
Just like you are.

The path

The path is important
only for the one walking on it.
But it doesn't have to be.

Membrane

Everything I see, hear, and feel,
experience,
is like a membrane,
infinitely thin,
between what sees
and what is seen.

What I am,
what sees,
on one side.
What is seen,
on the other.
Which is the same.

The membrane is the world,
like forms in it.
It is equally
what sees
and what is seen.
In the same now.

What sees,
sees only itself
as all forms,
as, of, and from itself,
without separation.

Every meeting
in the infinite and eternal
fusion
of seeing and the seen,
is what all this is.

True?

Mischa is not true.
Truth is Mischa.

Dare to test this!

The music is streamed from the internet to your electronic device.
But the volume is turned all the way down, so you don't hear anything.
But the music is obviously still streamed, "in the air".

Surely, you understand that the music still is there, regardless of you experiencing it or not. Surely, you also understand that if your body were to have different organs that could translate the signals "in the air" into an experience of music, you would experience music.

Can you now discover that the fact that you don't experience the music without such organs, has nothing to do with the music, but rather the limitations of your body? That what you experience is not "reality," but actually the limitations of your body?

Can you see that this also applies to the other bodily senses? Compare this to if the body were to lose these limitations:
If the body were to become weightless, spaceless, transparent…
Surely, you would then have many experiences that you cannot have with the limitations.
Isn't it the same way with the limitations of the mind?

Can you see that this also applies to what is happening in and through the mind, that the experience is not of reality, but the limitations of the mind? And that if the mind were to be freed from its limitations, you would experience more and different things?

Maybe a humility appears regarding your own perceptions of reality, when you realize that it is the limitations of mind and not reality that determine what you perceive as reality.

Are you open to the possibility of letting go of the perceptions that are based on the limitations of the mind?
Are you open to the possibility that mind can grow and expand, so that you can experience more of reality, and more true to reality?

If you can see this, I believe you can also see and feel – through everything described above and everything else in life – that the mind consists of that which always is and always has been the same, and is that which experiences everything, including your mind… that it is what you actually Are… and that the "everything else" actually is the limitations of the body and mind.

When your mind is informed by this, actually the only True, I also believe that it is fully possible that your actions in the world – the world that looks the way it does due to the limitations that are believed to define reality – will change, will become more humble and reverent before the Reality that you now realize is much more that what you previously thought.

And if you were to dare taking yet another step, even closer to Reality…

If you were to try separating yourself from the experience, whether it is a day at work, deep sleep, or coma – what would that look like? Would it even be possible? If not, the irrefutable and only conclusion is:

You are what you experience. You are therefore the World! Including the teacup on the table, and your own mind, with everything it contains, and everything in between and around.

It just might be more exciting now, in a deeper and more intimate way,
to explore the World…!

Say!
Don't say what you think, say what your heart is.

Death?
Life contains both birth and death,
but never dies itSelf.

I am. Life.
That which contains both birth and death.

Two worlds?
Cross your eyes, and you see two worlds.
Some would say that you see two realities.

But no, it is One reality,
which is one with Seeing.

The seeing that dances with Reality,
dancing in itSelf, a dance that is all this.

You are Seeing and Reality.
The same Reality that sees. ItSelf.

Shadows

Phenomena that appear in what I Am,
regardless if they are
powerful experiences or not,
can be called shadows that are formed
in My light.
A mistake is often made
when a phenomenon feels good,
and when it is believed to be Truth.

Phenomena are phenomena,
and they come and go,
but I Am always what I Am.
If I believe that phenomena are Truth,
I can actually end up
in very unpractical and
even dangerous situations.

Psychological maturity, common sense,
and spiritual discernment are tools
that can be used to prevent this.
Then, phenomena can live in what I Am,
not the other way around.
Peace.

Permanent

Whatever happens,
changes the mind,
or rather: The mind changes,
just like everything else changes.

The mind is never as it once was.
Therefore, it does not define what I am.
If something permanent is experienced,
it cannot be the mind.

The only permanent,
is to be and to experience,
to experience also the changing mind,
which does not define the permanent.

Judging

Chinese proverb:
He who blames others
has a long way to go on his journey.
He who blames himself
is halfway there.
He who blames no one
has arrived.

Luke 6:37
Judge not, and ye shall not be judged:
condemn not, and ye shall not be condemned:
forgive, and ye shall be forgiven.

In light of the understanding that I am
nothing else than Consciousness
manifesting as what I call the "I,"
just like every other "I" –
how can I judge anyone?
Someone who is nothing else
than what I am…

The years go by, but not I

What I am, is what was the 5-year old
who scraped his knee, and the 40-year old
who had a son.

Neither the 5-year old nor the 40-year old
exist anymore, but that which was them,
is always here, now and tomorrow.

Neither the 5-year old nor the 40-year old
was what always is the same, but what is
always the same, was them.

What always is the same, is the same that
was you, and is what we are now.

About synchronicity*

To try to achieve or experience synchronicity by becoming "more spiritual"
is to confuse the relative and absolute.

In spiritual circles, it is reported that synchronicity happens more often to those that are "more spiritual". But this can be seen in many ways, in varying proportions:

- With greater acceptance of what happens along the path, it is more likely that things that happen are liked and that they correspond more to the attitude you have.

- It is said that "you see what you want to see". And we tend to not remember other things.

- We really don't know. And nothing in the relative changes what we really are. With this attitude, maybe it somehow opens up for nice things to happen, but old knowledge doesn't necessarily have anything to do with it, rather "living in the now" does.

To find evidence for what is often claimed – "what happens in the relative is affected by my personal spiritual development" – is difficult or impossible, and there is so much room for personal interpretations that, maybe, that's all it is.

Personally:
If I think that I see synchronicity happen, this question can appear in me: "For whom or what are things favorable – if at all?" Then it usually happens that these things don't occupy my attention any longer.

Un-findable

If science cannot find anything substantial, solid, or real when they drill down into matter and only find space and quantum soup, or when they look out into the universe and cannot look further than the event horizon…

…is it not quite comical that we can believe that if we only could look carefully enough, we would find the essence of man, something substantial, solid, or real… in the body or brain?

Police?

Always on guard.
Always someone or something
that is wrong and must be changed.
I constantly have to go into
situations where I am right,
or know better what to do.
To find the one to blame
for my experience.
Police. That is my job,
every day.

Or?

So many are feeling so bad,
what can I do?
Comfort a little here,
encourage some there.
Tell about other ways,
different ways to see?
What is called "me"
is the sum of everything
and everyone's experience of "me" –
so what else can I do,
or be…?
Servant. That is my desire, my calling.
In the infinite and eternal Love
that is the open reality of everything,
mine, too – how could I be anything else?

When we see each other for what we are,
instead of each other's faults,
and everything that should be different,
what happens then?

Do we see that we're all in the same boat,
on the same journey,
a journey we seldom know much about?
That we actually can let others
have their faults and shortcomings,
just like we can have ours?

And that what we all need
and long for, is already with us
on our collective journey?
Maybe even "within us"?

Can we then be to each other
precisely what we all need?
We are probably free to be this,
because reality does not interfere.

"Owe no man any thing,
but to love one another,"
said an old guru.
Already then.

In a time of universal deceit,
telling the truth is a revolutionary act.

George Orwell? (1903 – 1950)

From within

The world
presents itself
exactly as we see it.

It seems like there are
individual ways
to view one finite world.

But in reality,
there is only infinite Awareness
experiencing individual views.

See the world
from within Awareness,
and experience your Self.

See and hear

It is not light that makes it possible to see.
It is Seeing.

It is not sound that makes it possible to hear.
It is Hearing.

(Seeing and Hearing have many "siblings,"
but it's the same way with all of them)

Seeing cannot be seen,
and Hearing cannot be heard,
but they see and hear everything,
at the same time. This.
All this.

What is seen
is not Seeing.
What is heard
is not Hearing.

Conform

It is said that one sees only one's own mind.
It is clearly exemplified by this:
You realize that whatever you see,
is a construction made by your own mind,
because someone else looking at the same scene
sees things differently.

So, in this regard we can definitely establish
that what you see, is your own mind's construction of it.
And that is not reality.
Reality contains every perspective that any being can have.

If you believe yourself to be a separate entity,
and that what you see is reality,
then reality will "conform" to the way you see.
If you believe yourself to be simply Awareness,
then reality will conform itself to that way of seeing.

Beauty

You look at a beautiful picture.
The picture is a gateway to the experience of beauty.
It is as though, if you were actually there when the picture was taken,
you would experience beauty –
the same beauty that you experienced when looking at a beautiful picture,
the beauty that is always the same,
and independent of the items, events or people in the picture,
and of the time and space in between them.
And you have just realized:
Beauty is always where and what you are.
Seemingly forgetting that, does not make it any other way,
since you are always the same beauty.

See Venice and then die?

The director Luchino Visconti in the documentary *The most beautiful boy in the world* (2021) about the movie *Death in Venice* (1971):

–"This kind of Death, it's an intellectual Death, you know, it's a story about an intellectual who follows the Beauty, the absolute Beauty in the world, and when he finds it in a young boy who lives at the Grand Hôtel des Bains, and you know, when he puts his eyes on the Beauty, he puts the eyes on the Death."

When one sees absolute Beauty, one also sees Death. When absolute Beauty is seen, there is no more. In a very deep sense, this is Death. In seeing absolute Beauty, the subject and the object are no more.

The movie

I am playing the lead character in this movie,
the movie that I am watching right now.
You are playing the lead character in the movie,
the movie that you are watching right now.
Somebody else is playing the lead character in the movie,
the movie that he is watching right now.
The thing is that it is the same movie, and the experience of it
is what this text is describing:
That I am playing the lead character…
you are playing the lead character… etc.

When I realize this, that everything behaves this way, I also see this:
You, I, and somebody else are the same, the same that experiences
both you, me, and someone else in the same movie.

I see this, and I feel that actually, in all seriousness, I am what is happening in the movie,
whether it affects you, me, or someone else – and that what is experiencing the movie
is completely unaffected.

If I see every event in my life as a frame in the movie that I'm currently watching,
maybe I see this, too:

If I were to want that the movie should be different in some way,
I can remind myself that the absolutely only movie that exists, is this one!

Then there are no "other" or different movies – that nobody is watching –
and they have no importance at all, for no other reason that they don't exist.
Why else?

First and foremost because the only movie that exists,
is precisely this one, and it is where and what I am.
How could I but love and care for everything in it?

A riddle?

You are. You are what you are.
Absolutely independently of what you – what you are – experience.

To find out exactly what you are, is therefore the highest endeavor one can make,
because all else is hinging on this discovery, revelation, or insight.

No one can tell you what you are. Only What-You-Are can know, see, feel what you are.
It follows then, that you cannot tell anyone what you are, and much less tell someone
else what they are.

Environment

Man is amazed
and is driven to more research when it is discovered
how an animal species changes their environment,
by the use of tools, for example.
This driving force is probably partly in order to
explore the origin of man, that is to say, himself.

Maybe we could be more amazed,
and instead just learn from this,
that animal species most often do not change their environment at all,
and maybe this could tell us something important.
Maybe we can realize that we don't need to change it much, either,
like we do so frantically and often without regard
of neither our own environment nor each other.

Ego?

Insofar as we can talk about an ego, it is more of an activity.
The ego is thus more of a "consequence" of seeing, than of how it sees.
If the world is viewed as an enemy, "the ego" acts on that.
If the world is viewed as oneself, "the ego" acts on that.
It seems like we don't "get rid of" the ego in earthly life.
The ego is thus more of a faithful servant than a master, lord, or leader.
Everything I see, also the ego, is the wake of what I am.

Patience

Patience is the accepting to wait for something unknown. Even the next moment is
unknown, and this is how patience is our nature. Impatience is the forgetting of our
nature. When the unknown becomes known, impatience is revealed for what it is:
Nothing but an idea in the mind, an idea that was heavy to bear. When it is seen for
what it is, it is gone, like the morning mist at sunrise.

Order of magnitude

Mind uses the brain
in order to perceive the world.
The brain does not,
and cannot use mind.

It is the same above, in an order of magnitude* "up":

Consciousness uses mind
in order to see Itself as the world.
Mind does not,
and cannot use Consciousness.

About space and time

About space:
Here exists, it is experienced.
There does not exist, it is not experienced.
What it is like to be Here is known.
What it is like to be There is unknown,
and only speculation.
When I am There,
it is still the same Here.
There is only a construction of thought
that assumes that There exists,
and is therefore circular reasoning.

About time:
Now exists, it is experienced.
Then and *Before* do not exist, they are not experienced.
What it is like Now is known.
What it is like Then and Before is unknown,
and only speculation and memory.
When I am Then, it is still the same Now.
When I was Before, it was still the same Now.
Then and *Before* are only constructions of thought
that assumes that they exist,
and is therefore circular reasoning.

Knowing

A chair does not know that it is a chair,
and cannot know it either.
A computer does not know that it is a computer,
and cannot know it either.
But knowing knows that a human is a human,
one called "you," one called "me," etc.
What is it that knows, then?
It cannot be the human that knows,
because knowing only knows
of something other than what it is.
Knowing knows about things:
The chair, the computer, the human…
And knowing knows that it knows.

If we approach knowing even closer…
Is it really known that a chair is a chair,
that a computer is a computer,
and that a human is a human?
A chair is a chair, a computer is a computer,
a human is a human,
only in human though.
And knowing knows about these thoughts,
so knowing cannot be a thought either.
Knowing also knows when there is nothing to know,
like in dreamless deep sleep and general anesthesia.
So the only real knowing,
that which really knows, is knowing.
It is what only remains.
Knowing, that which has knowing.
Consciousness.

The falling tree

The question is not
if there is a sound of a falling tree
when no one is there to hear it.
The question is not if what we experience
is real or not.

The answer lies again in the question.
The fact that everyone agrees on,
is that we all experience the same,
and this is because we are
the selfsame Self that experiences.

When we hear the same falling tree,
and when we experience anything together,
it is because we are the same,
not because the things are real,
but because that which experiences them is real.

That which experiences is the reality
of both that which experiences and
what is experienced, regardless of
whether one or many hear the sound of a falling tree
or have any experience at all.

The searching

Scientists are searching continuously,
they hope to find what we consist of
and what constitutes a human being,
but they only find cells, molecules, atoms…
but above all, they do not find what is searching.

But they definitely know and feel
that they are what is searching.
And it is self-evident
that what is searching
cannot be something that is searched for.

What is searching precedes what is searched for,
the searching is always too late, behind.
Therefore, that which is searching cannot be
something that originated from
what is searched for.

We have not forgotten

We have not forgotten what we are or where we came from.
We lack nothing that we seek to become complete, whole.
How is it, then?
Well, like this – and it cannot be any other way:
We are this.
This is what we look like now.
What it looks like now is not set in stone.
We really only know one thing about this "world":
It changes, it is not persistent, it happens,
and we are what it happens in, because we are that which experiences it.
And it looks like this – and includes that someone is searching
for something that he believes is lacking.
Even that is a possible form in what is.

So if we only are what we are,
then our propensity to help someone in distress, for example,
is not governed by our personal memories of what it is like to be in distress,
but we are informed by knowing that we also are the one in distress,
and then we make available to him all that we can,
so that he is no longer in distress, regardless of who he is.
This charity is not personal.

There are many noble contributions in the world
that are financed by appealing
to the personal empathy for the distressed,
and the organizer is often elevated as a benefactor.
But these actions do not lead to
the end of suffering for humanity,
but only for those who are allowed to enjoy for a moment,
a personally directed and therefore limited charity.

The charity that is informed by the understanding
that we are that which all distress is happening in,
a charity that is called "god's mercy" in the religions,
which is considered to be much larger than the charity of individual persons,
this charity is in fact what we all are and consist of,
and therefore it is not personal, and it contains everything we experience.
Even someone who is searching for something that he believes is lacking,
and even someone in distress.

Purpose?

Question: –So this philosophy, this world view,
speaks a lot about that there is no purpose
for really anything that happens in the world?
Answer: –The very notion, the question of purpose,
is what creates, not only purpose,
but also futility – at the same time.

It is not that there is either purpose or futility
in what we see in the world –
there are only things, actions, and minds,
and views of them, from different perspectives.
What we are, is all that.
Complete.

The same goes for love and fear,
good and evil, good and bad.
And it always holds true:
All notions create its shadow.
Knowing that I am all that,
I can rest in peace.

Being is the reality of achieving.
Being is the reality of failure.
Being is the reality of everything –
reward and burden, pride and shame –
and nothing defines or changes being,
only the content of experience.

Informed by this realization,
the person that I also am
will probably think and act differently
from when I was not informed by it.
Now I see and feel
that I am also my neighbor.

Parable: A human being is a sensor

A sensor sits on a network of sensors.
This sensor does not know what the other sensors are registering.
But the sensor does not really know anything, it only registers something.

The knowledge of what is registered is actually the consciousness that experiences what the sensor registers, yes, what all the sensors in the network register.

That the sensor can imagine that it is the sensor that experiences what is registered, is in fact the same consciousness that experiences what all sensors are registering. The network of sensors, the whole network, is something that consciousness uses to experience the world.

It can feel scary
to hear that what I am
is the consciousness itself
in the experience of seeing, for example,
and that it is the same consciousness
that sees everything else –
scary only if I am of the opinion
that seeing ceases when the sensor stops working.
But we already know
that seeing does not cease, it goes on,
even when "my" particular sensor stops working.

There is no separate sensor,
no alone sensor outside of the network,
because then there would be no experience
of what that sensor registers.
The fact that experience is happening,
points to several undoubtable things:

1. All sensors are in the same network.
2. I am in reality that which experiences, not the sensor.
3. You are nothing else than this, either.

God sleeps in the rock, dreams in the plant, stirs in the animal, and awakens in man.

Ibn Arabi (1165–1240)

Short version about what has happened:

I walked around and lived in this world, we can call it the circus. Naturally, I understood a lot about it, how it works, etc, and that I, my person also is a part of the same circus. But honestly, I did not understand it fully, not how things work and interact, how they are interconnected, what all the details mean and how I could best relate to them. Not that I hadn't really tried to understand it, for I really did so in many different ways. Not to mention all the different opinions about this circus! From experts and scientists to all the sects that pop up now and then, one not like the other, and many of them trying to market their view as the best one, or most real one, from time to time.

Then it happened all of a sudden, when I sat pondering all this regarding the circus, it felt sort of like I fell backward and landed in what is on "this side" of the whole circus, including my person. I had believed that I and the world was the whole circus, and that there was nothing else, and that I was in the middle of it and a part of it, just like everyone else, so to speak. But right then, it was as though I ended up, not behind or outside, but on this side of the experience of the whole circus, in a "place" that I did not know existed. Here, it was completely still. Nothing changed about or in the circus, but in this stillness, it was as though I saw both the person who I thought I was and the whole circus – but from a place where I only saw and understood, without being involved or affected, and without any inner commentator that used to always comment and evaluate everything.

Something dawned on me – not about the circus or the person that I thought was all I was – no, I saw and felt that what I am is on this side of both the circus and the person, this side of everything. And here, I could look at the circus – including the person that I am in it – in a brand new way. Completely without doubt or faith, I felt that what I really am, is what is here, on this side of everything, and that neither the person in the circus nor what happens in the circus can affect what I now feel and know that I am.

It may sound like I, at that moment, distanced myself from, took a step away from the circus, but it was the other way around – the circus, including the person that I am in it, happens within what I really am. Before, I saw other persons and things that happen in the circus as things that were outside me, and now it was the other way around. Everything happens so near me and intimately in me – not in the person that I also am, the person in the circus, but in what I now feel and see that I really am, on this side of it all.

I don't care anymore? (Self inquiry)

I am blaming myself for feeling like I don't care anymore. Others have even almost accused me of not caring anymore. The difficulty can seem to be to forgive myself for feeling this way, and to allow myself to feel this way.

But this does not mean that forgiving myself is what I should do. Instead, I can realize that it doesn't matter whether I feel this way or not. So the difficulty I experience, is really the blaming of myself.

More than this, I can also realize that there is no higher or lower way to feel about this than the way I feel, including having difficulty with blaming myself for feeling this way. Blaming myself does not change or affect what I really am; that which experiences it all.

But: Is this a cop-out? The conclusion of the above, does not really explain or address anything, nor does it give license to myself feeling like this, nor to blaming myself. And what I really Am is open to, and has no problem with the possibility that I continue feeling this way, nor with blaming myself for it.

Finding out what this feeling really is, is to also find out that it doesn't matter. And I could be fooling myself into thinking that it's okay to have this difficulty – which it also is!

I can surmise that the above perspective can be seen as that of Consciousness. It is always nice to know what I am, and to be that Consciousness, to which every experience is closer than myself, yet does not change or affect it.

But:
What about the perspective of the person, this mind, in which all the difficulty is felt? Or rather, the mind is the difficulty, the difficulty consists of only mind.

In all of this, I am not avoiding the question about feeling this way, that I don't care anymore. Feeling this way does feel bad, and I can learn from investigation what this feeling really is. I could be focusing on the difficulty with blaming myself, but I will not look at that, I will look at what it is like to feel that I don't care anymore. Is it true that my person does not care anymore? Is this what my person really feels?

I remember that I already understand that feeling a certain way, can very well be based on things that are not true, and if I later find this out, I don't feel that way any longer.

This questioning of myself does not make "two" out of me. All there really is, is Consciousness that experiences and expresses itself, here as a person who may feel that he doesn't care anymore and blames himself for it.

So, as this Consciousness, I can ask my person about this. Consciousness is, as it were, talking to the manifestation in itself.

So I ask: "Do you feel like you don't care anymore?" When I hear this question, deep down I feel "No I don't, of course I care," but in the mind this thought is born, that says: "Yes, I don't care anymore," but since my person has difficulty feeling this way, it is said with a degree of shame. The difficulty and shame is not really about feeling that way, but about the blaming of myself, and that blaming is due to a clash between what is true and what is not true. What is true, is that I always care, but not about what I do or what happens, but about doing what I care about. So what I could be telling myself, is to continue doing what I care about. And then the real question becomes: "What do I care about?"

It could also be the case that I, the person, is starting to feel more like from what I really Am, which cannot say "I care" or "I don't care," since both are possible expressions of itself. As I am feeling more and more what is True, I feel that what is True is not dependent on whether my person cares or not. When I feel this, thoughts appear afterward, about it being wrong to not care. An emotion consists of a thought plus a story, and so it feels uncomfortable or wrong to "not care," but the emotion is not connected to what it would feel like to not care, the discomfort is felt because what is felt ("I don't care") is not aligned with what is True, namely that it doesn't matter whether I care or not.

This reasoning with myself lands in this:

I don't care about what I do.
I do what I care about.

About dreaming

An obvious basis for being able to carry on a sensible conversation with someone about the content of my dreams, is that I am well aware that I am not the dreamed character, but the dreamer, and that the content of the dream, including the dreamed character, consists solely of my mind.

The same basis for being able to carry on a sensible conversation with someone about the content of my waking experiences, is that I am well aware that I am not any of the content of what is experienced – including my body and brain – but that which experiences. The content of what is experienced consists solely of that which experiences it.

My dreaming probably is the way it is because it is a reflection of – and reminder of – what my whole person consists of.

Obvious

One thing is so obvious when we are not on the same page.
Not because of what it true or not, nor right or wrong.
How we speak is an expression of how we see.
One way of seeing is in itself neither better nor worse than any other way.
Neither does it have to with what is seen:
In me, you can see an enemy or someone lovable.
Neither of those ways of seeing are true in themselves.
What is seen, is a construction of different minds,
which depends on how we see.
Someone is making himself an image of what he believes is reality,
and someone else is making himself a different image of what he believes is reality,
in spite of them seeing the same reality.
The image of one does not correspond to the image of another.
Disagreement may arise, or something worse,
not because the one is right and the other wrong.
Before right and wrong, before someone sees an enemy in me or someone lovable,
before what is seen, and before how it is seen,
there is but one real and true:
The seeing itself.
Seeing makes no difference between good and bad seeing,
good and bad person or event.
Seeing only sees.

That which sees

That which sees an apple on the table is real, it is here, it is present.
But that which sees, cannot be seen. Thus far, most of us agree.

But take another step.

When we stand in front of each other and we look into our eyes,
that which sees me is that which sees you.

Consciousness is not personal

Consciousness is not personal because we are all conscious in exactly the same way. Not only that, we are all conscious in exactly the same now. We know this, for example when we do video chats through both timezones and the date line.

It is easy to conclude that "the one's consciousness" looks identical to, behaves identically with, and is identical to the other's. Not only that, we are all conscious of the same. No one has the same story as anyone else, and not the same perception about the content in consciousness, but if we peel off the story and the perceptions about the content in consciousness, there is only consciousness left – and it is not only common, it is the same, identical.

That it is the same consciousness, makes it so that when two persons smell the same rose, the experiencing is the same, and we see that it is so. That we experience the same, is not because it is the same rose and the same fragrance, but because we are the same that experiences. The bodily senses may be different, one may be deaf, the other blind, but this text is not about that. It is about how what is experienced simultaneously clearly points to consciousness not being personal, and that it is the same consciousness that is conscious of the same reality.

Whatever it is that makes us believe that it is two different and separate experiences – e.g. different bodily senses, perceptions, etc. – we can put that aside for a while and conclude that the experience is not two, and that it is one and the same consciousness that experiences the same reality.

If we expound on this, it also means that even if one experiences something in Sweden, and the other something in Brazil, what is experiencing "through" both, is still identical. The content of experience does not change that which experiences.

Taking sides

The question of taking sides does not live in me. I understand how this question arises in the land of Right&Wrong, but I don't live there. It may sound like I am making things too easy for myself this way, but it is the other way around. We have been taught so well that we must take one side, stand up for one's opinions, assert influence through party politics, etc. But remember that every side, behind every standpoint, everyone holds on to something that they **believe** is true. Everyone believes that they are on the right side, and they try to get me and others to join it. There has to be something crazy with all this. When I look around, no one has really succeeded, either. The fact that more and more fractions of standpoints occur, does not make things easier.

Naturally, most of us mean well, only a very few have taken extremely exclusive and deviant positions. Is it possible for everyone to gather around what we all feel the same about, instead? That no one should have to go without food and drink, that we all should be able to live without lack and violence? And in this way stand on everyone's side, because it is the same – and really no one's side, but the same. Can we still not comprehend that what stands in the way for everyone getting a liveable life is precisely… sides, opinions, parties, egotism, nationalism, ethnocentrism, etc. Whatever stands in the way is conditioned and learned – and can be unconditioned and unlearned! In oneself. Now. Nowhere else, and at no other time.

Love of wisdom

The original meaning of the word philosophy seems to have been completely neglected in our culture. When did we last hear about wisdom at all, in economy, politics, etc? Wisdom is something that comes from something deeper and closer to us than knowledge. Have we learned to believe that if we only acquire a certain measure of knowledge about everything, we will solve all the problems in the world? When would that measure be full, then? And how should it be determined?

Wisdom is something other than knowledge. Someone may possess all knowledge and yet completely lack wisdom, and the wisest can be very unknowledgeable. Wise comes from the sanskrit *vedas* and means to see, to see in an active sense, to see what the circumstances are, and what needs to be done. This seeing does not require having knowledge of the past. If someone is seen who is about to die of hunger or thirst, the acting becomes automatic; to assist with food and drink. It is **wise** to do so. Therefore, if assistance is not provided when one or millions of starving people are seen – something must be standing in the way of wisdom. It is actually completely irrelevant to know about anything else, not even about what stands in the way, or having the knowledge about the history of a people, their financial or political situation, how an assistance of food and drink may affect the ones assisting, etc. If someone lacks food and drink, we assist with food and drink, end of story. Surely, we can feel that it is wisdom, a clear and unfiltered seeing, that we are lacking – and not knowledge.

This text was born while pondering how it is that I am not drawn to social activism.

Gruesome truth

Hatred, anger, revengefulness –
we can see that these are actually Love misdirected, but turned 180°,
and that they look like forgetfulness of truth.
And they do not feel like love, nor forgetfulness,
they feel exactly like hatred, anger, and revengefulness.
And that is to feel like never having felt love.

For it to be possible to feel this love, like having never not felt it,
every hatred, anger, and revengefulness must also be felt,
and the forgetting of truth.
To feel this love and remembrance of truth,
there also comes with it, like the other side of a coin,
the feeling like never having felt love.

The whole universe operates identically.
For there to be a force, an opposing force is required,
so that in the big picture, nothing has really changed.
The harmony and balance is perfect and eternally unperturbed,
as energy contains both force and opposing force.
But in the big picture, nothing has ever really changed it.

For there to be wealth, poverty is required.
For there to be health, sickness is required.
When seeing them as good and bad, good and evil,
the selfish driving force will be toward achieving wealth and health –
at the expense of the poor and the sick,
by reason of this misdirected Love, turned 180°.

So the idea that Earth's population could live in peace and equality,
where everyone is provided for, is not possible at all,
unless each one of us wakes up to truth, that our essence is
what contains and experiences wealth and health, poverty and sickness.
In other words, harmony and balance lies only in clearly seeing
that neither wealth nor poverty, neither health nor sickness
defines us, and that harmony and balance is what we are,
in which everything takes place.

Clearly seeing this, there will be no selfish driving force
toward achieving wealth and health
at the expense of the poor and sick –
and everything can effortlessly be distributed fairly,
in a truly just and equal fashion,
without fear of loss or injustice.

On the ideological scale today, we have the extremes,
both capitalism that enables the very few to own and exploit the very many,
and communism that forces the population through taxes and labor
to enable the very few to rule and live off the very many.
These two, then, are de facto the same.
And we remember that it is actually Love misdirected, turned 180°.

Only after clearly seeing that our essence is what contains it all,
and that nothing that is experienced defines what we are,
the selfish driving force toward wealth and health will cease.
Therefore, the highest and most holy ambition
in everyone's heart, not only should be,
but have to be, to clearly see, feel, and act on this.

Simple as pie

When we are together, I see you and you see me. You are the seeing that sees me. I am
also the seeing that sees me. I am the seeing that also sees you. Not because we are two
who see each other, but because we are the same seeing. You are the seeing, and I am
the same seeing.

When you and I look at an apple together, you are the seeing that sees an apple. I am
also the seeing that sees an apple. But here comes a cat! The cat would not say that it
sees an apple, but it sees what we see. It is also the seeing that sees what we see, just like
you and I are. Not because a cat, you, and I see the same thing, but we see the same
thing because we are the same seeing.

When we are not together you see a coffeecup on your table, but I see a teacup on my
table. If the cat is with you, it would not say that it sees a coffeecup, but it sees what you
see. The cat, you, and I are the same seeing, even if you see something other than what I
see. The seeing is not changed because the cat and you see a coffeecup on your table
and I see a teacup on my table – it is still the same seeing.

It is the same way with all seeing, even for a blind person who sees neither form nor
color. I am, you are, the cat is, and the blind person is the same seeing, even though we
don't see the same thing, or anything at all.

It is the same way with all perception. **That which perceives** is the same. And what is
perceived does not change **that which perceives**.

My grandfather's father perceived when the radio came to his village. I do not. Yet we
are the same seeing, because my grandfather's father and I are **that which sees**.

It has been said that we cannot see **that which sees**. This is correct, my person cannot see **that which sees**, it is not my body or person that sees, but makes it possible for **what I Am** to see. What I Am, is also what you Are. When we look at a sunset, a sailboat, or an apple, **that which sees** sees what is seen.

Something interesting happens when we meet, we the "instruments" of seeing, two bodies and persons. In this meeting, it is fully possible to be reminded that **What sees**, sees itSelf. When you see me, you see that I see you, and vice versa, but because we are the same seeing, it is in fact the seeing that sees itSelf. To another person, this can be perceived as intimidating and too intimate – not to **that which sees**, but to that person.

Actually, it is really no different when I listen to what you say, because **that which hears** is in fact equally intimate with **that which speaks**. Perhaps it is a bit more difficult to be reminded that **What is speaking** is **What is hearing**, but it is exactly the same way about speaking and hearing. In the same way, it is fully possible to be reminded that when I touch you, it is really impossible to divide this experience in two, because when I touch your hand, it is equally and simultaneously you touching my hand. **That which feels** you, is **that which feels** me, it is the same sensing. What makes sensing, hearing, speaking, and seeing possible only looks like two bodies and persons, but is in reality the same. When we love each other, it is the same Love that loves itSelf. It is wonderful to be reminded of this.

CHAPTER 4

Nothing

This space is intentionally left empty.

Spring, 2019. Through many solar revolutions, we have met and fellowshipped in an intense frenzy and euphoria, in the discovery of what we really are. But the creativity in this unorganized group that we seemed to be, ebbs out and the activities cease rather quickly, as I see it. Maybe this cannot be explained, but I don't seek an explanation either. Neither do I know what will come after, if anything. Nothing remains of the group, so to speak.

I explore this "nothing," and indeed, a lot is written about that, too, even though it seems absolutely impossible. In the exploration, after "approaching" this Nothing, the intellect collapses, and nothing meaningful can really be constructed about it. In several analogies, it is described that when the moth so longs to experience the flame, the only way to do so… is to be consumed by it, to be annihilated.

"Nothing" is a mystical concept that starts to fascinate me. Not for its potential to stimulate the intellect, but because experience seems to contain "more" – as if the concept "Consciousness" does not fully describe that which is experiencing.

In this context, it is also curious that we have gotten the zero in mathematics from the Arabic culture, not the Roman. Maybe the zero was an expression of that the Arabic culture and philosophy was open to the possibility that "nothing" is real and even the origin of what is not nothing?

In the fall of 2020, I go through an operation under general anesthesia induced by the now commonly used substance propofol. I took the opportunity to explore the experience of being, under general anesthesia and the waking up from it. I ask the anesthesiologist for two things before the operation:

"Tell me exactly when you inject the substance" and "Tell me exactly when you stop injecting me, and when it's time to wake up." He thinks this is an interesting philosophical experiment and does so.

In deep sleep, there seems to be a vague experience that becomes part of the episodic memory, that I have slept well after having had the needed amount of periods of deep sleep, and I can imagine that these periods are still experienced, that I have been aware of "nothing," an emptiness, or absence of things.

But after the propofol anesthesia, it is clear to me that in what Is, there is also the possibility to not experience at all.

The organism "human" is apparently a combination of mind and body, and sometimes this organism is called "body-mind". Without mind, the body dies, this is known. A living body is in this regard dependent on the mind, but nothing can be said about the mind being dependent on a body.

My body is put under on the operating table and the mind is present, since the body does not die. That which experiences my mind and body is also present, obviously, or rather, everything experienced happen "in" that which experiences. And something is present when the body is no longer injected with propofol, and my mind "wakes up" intact.

To experience can be likened to a movie that consists of a number of frames. In deep sleep, it seems that several frames are black or empty – but they are still part of the movie, and I remember the experience of them. Under general anesthesia though, there are no frames at all, not even black or empty ones. To fall asleep happens on one frame, and waking up happens on the next frame. This matches perfectly the other two occasions where I was put under with the same substance, although I did not reflect on the experience then.

That which experiences, obviously experiences continually, regardless if it is "through" my body-mind or someone else's. How used we are to thinking that Consciousness somehow is separate and occurring in and is present inside my body-mind! But again, it is 180° from this. Reversed.

The body-mind that is called Mischa is experienced. All his thoughts, emotions, and perceptions are experienced "through," or **as** that body-mind. The Mischa-body-mind is a "localized precipitation" in, from, and by that which experiences it. Mischa can be likened to one of many whirlpools in a river, where all the whirlpools consist of the same water, the same river that contains and experiences all the whirlpools, even if the "whirlpool Mischa" is absolutely still during general anesthesia. But that which experiences is in no way dependent on him, on the contrary, he is completely dependent on that which experiences – without that which experiences, no Mischa. And no one else or anything else either.

In the different sciences, when they look for Consciousness, it is assumed that the body or the person **has** a consciousness that is separate from other persons' consciousness – but it is not so, it is Consciousness that contains and experiences all the bodies and persons. Often, consciousness and what one is conscious **of** is equated. But Consciousness obviously does not cease to be, does not end, when nothing is experienced.

Scientists always put the cart before the horse, and they do not realize that Consciousness is primary. They look for the actor in the television, to use another analogy. The question "Where does consciousness arise?" is the wrong question – everything arises in Consciousness.

Complete void

The void must be void, also, of voidness.

Wei Wu Wei (1895–1986)

I am
erases itself

Because I am this,
it is I
that this happens in, from, and by,
which is this,
that I am.
But since
it is I who am this…
What is it then
that experiences this,
that describes this,
with precisely these words?

This question hurts so much,
and is so unpleasant,
because the answer implies the end
of all that I am.
To not exist,
in the Great Void.
So what I am,
is then also to not exist.
So it's cool!

It is also cool to exist.
Until I see that I don't.
Then it might be difficult
to think, feel, experience,
or to do anything at all!
Until I see
that it is I who does it.
Then I am this.

Da Capo Non Fine

Stillness

Now, stillness.
As always.
Nothing happens
when the struggle is over.
To just be.
Without seeking pleasure,
it is just nice.
Love in fullness.
Empty of everything.

Where everything went
doesn't matter.
How the struggle ended,
I know nothing about.
What happens now,
is just this.
All movement
comes and goes
in the stillness.

To only know and feel,
that here, I belong,
here, is all of me,
all I have ever been.
What has become,
changes nothing.
In all the ripples,
and all the storm waves of the ocean,
I am Ocean.

Ten thousand things

I see that all ten thousand things
are forms in me,
including my body and mind,
and all emptiness, all fullness,
and all spaces in between.

The ten thousand things are really myself,
being conscious of all this,
from every perspective.

Beyond consciousness is the indescribable,
in which consciousness
of ten thousand things occur,
where nothing fills all of its emptiness,
and nothing happens.

Worlds are born and die in consciousness,
which never dies,
and that in turn,
is the indescribable
nothing.

Flow

When the mind's compulsion to run things
ceases, things can happen in a natural flow
from the Void, the Unknown, Emptiness.

Silence

The sound you hear when I speak,
is born from silence.
All that comes from silence,
or ever could come from it,
is hearing and sound.
All you hear when I speak,
are sounds of silence.
All I speak when you hear,
are sounds of silence.

How can I say this?
Because the sound is not the hearing,
and not the speaking.
Therefore, the hearing and speaking
come from silence.

And when you hear my speaking,
we both agree that we experience
hearing and speaking.
Therefore, we must be
that non-hearing and non-speaking
silence.

Inseparable

We can see that all things seen,
are only reflections
of what Is.

To see this,
implies that what Is,
is also what we are.

To see this
and to be this,
is inseparable.

To be this
and to reflect this,
is inseparable.

To reflect this
and to see this,
is inseparable.

Give up

To give up is to let go.
Let go of all ideas
that I thought could hold me up.
I had simply forgotten
that I always am.

Now I see
that even letting go
is just wind.
A dream
that keeps the mind alive.

What could infinity
let go of?
What would timelessness need to do
to have time to be itself?
In this, everything appears, without effort.

Faith can move mountains,
if they are considered to be in the way.
Hope is a crutch of the mind,
when things don't go according to its plan.
The Love that I am, only sees.

It's time

Now it is time
to be picked clean
of everything and everyone.
To discover,
for real,
that I am
nothing,
out of and by which
everything appears.
Including "me".

So pleasurable

It is this pleasurable,
only because
it is this pleasurable.

It hurts this much,
only because
it hurts this much.

Simultaneously,
what I am,
is all this.

Regardless of
what it is or does,
I am what I experience.

Maybe this is why
it is so pleasurable?
Would this not be enough?

If this would be enough
this understanding arrives,
of not being.

To be nothing
that appears as everything
that has a beginning and end.

To then not even be
anything nameable,
is to not be.

And now, out of what Is not,
the fragrance and sweetness
arises from… this.

Nothing alone

Alone.
When everything has ceased.
When everything is welcome,
discussions cease.
Nothing to be agitated about,
nothing to have opinions about.
Nothing to sell,
nothing to attract.

To be everything.
Blend in,
look like something.
Play and dance,
without anything at all
to claim.
No longer needing to be
something attractive.

Only see and welcome,
all that appears in itself,
does not attract,
but contains everything.
Nothing to analyze.
Nothing to evaluate.
Where nothing happens.
Such is alone.

The most beautiful,
where Nothing has a throne,
and Silence is singing.
Eternity looks
into this moment
and engorges it fully,
like a lover
who can never have enough.

The most powerful,
as I fade away
before the Terrible
which still gives me
this apparent existence,
yet for a while,
a flickering flame
in its infinite space.

My semblance is forever
on bended knees,
in the grace to be
Your handiwork,
in Your tireless cycles.
How can I or my errands,
diminish or exalt what You are,
the infinite and eternal that I taste?

No, I am the same Nothing,
out of which my form
only appears to flutter for a while,
singing that same song
that I have never not heard,
to dance that same dance,
that always owns my body.
Nothing is all form.

Alone.

It happens often that I sink so deeply into meditation that if someone were to watch me, he would say I am in trance.

It happens now and then, here and there that others, while being in trance, think it necessary or important to legitimize or validate what they have discovered, give it a higher status, for example by ascribing the discovery to a higher power or maybe some thousands year old spirit who "speaks through a messenger". In many circumstances, this has very unpleasant consequences – obedient followers, power play, embezzlement of money, etc. From my perspective, this is so incredibly unnecessary, because what is True stands on its own and needs no validation.

I say no, none of this alters what is True, regardless if it is told by an unassuming carpenter two thousand years ago or a modern leader of a cult.

The following is a text from after trance:

This is what Is that speaks. And hears.

Put aside all thoughts and concepts for a moment, to hear this.
My form barely dares to say it, since it is said also to this form.

If I can be the mouthpiece for a moment…
The mouthpiece that cannot exalt itself, not on this instrument.
You could say that this mouthpiece hears the same lovely tones that are produced,
even my little, little mouthpiece.

What I, the little mouthpiece, can say – even though it is much too beautiful
to pronounce – is that it is not the beauty of the mouthpiece that is reflected.
It is, it simply is.

It may sound presumptuous to ask if you are ready to hear, but with ready, I mean:
Be only hearing. Now.

It wants to be said to you, regardless if you listen or not,
regardless of what you are busy with or not, this:

**If what really Is
could say anything at all,
it is being said in precisely this way, right now.
This is what Is that speaks. And hears.**

It is now fully possible to look at the mouthpiece,
and to evaluate the sound that is heard.
To do so, would not change what Is, though,
because it is only what Is, that Is.
What Is, is both the speaking and the hearing.

It can look like a meeting
between what is spoken and what is heard.
And it can surely be experienced
that the speaking and the hearing is one and the same.
But you know already that you Are,
and that you already Are this,
and nothing else.

In this infinite, timeless, and formless,
and thus absolutely empty:
How could something appear out of it,
that is not what it consists of?
See this beauty, and also that you are it.
There is no one speaking,
and no one hearing,
but only this.

And if you for a moment would get an idea
that this would be the ultimate in passivity,
the pinnacle of navel-gazing, that's okay.
Let the idea come and go, just like everything else.
But surely you see, with your inner eye,
that this is the case, this is the way it is.
This is that.

And there is no difference. It is only this.
How could you be anything else than this?
You Are already!
And we completely agree that we Are this,
and that we cannot be anything else than this.

It is not practical that I speak forever, but I will never leave you,
because we can never be separate in this.
Yet, I want to remind you that when I speak and you listen,
absolutely nothing is actually happening,
it is the same nothing that can seem to appear as something
in this never ending cycle.
The absolute silence can seem to appear as this.
About this, it can also be said that there is one who speaks and one who hears.
But I am saying that it is the same.

The absolute silence, the absolute emptiness, seems to appear as this,
but it can seem to appear as everything that has already appeared, too,
and everything that appears now, and everything that will appear,
as seen from an illusory separate perspective.

What is surprising, is perhaps that what can also appear in this,
is the feeling of separation, to be abandoned, unloved, and whichever feeling.
And all that is just as welcome, naturally,
in, from, and by what really Is – as you are, and I am,
and the listening and the speaking Is.

The cycle is perfect, without beginning or end.
About that, it can be said, thought, and it can look like
that it is Being, swallowing its own tail.

Whatever and wherever in this cycle, and from every illusory perspective,
is perfectly welcome. Wherever in this cycle, it can feel every which way,
and that anything can happen – or rather, that is what is happening already.

It can also happen, that the cycle is confused about what it appears in, that is to say,
what I started to talk about, that which really Is. It can even look like this is about to
end, but it does not.

Thank you, thank you for everything!
But first and foremost, thank you for nothing, for it appearing…
as this. That you and I Are.

Sound of silence

Exactly every sound
must come out of silence.
Everything that can be said, written, described,
about precisely "this,"
is this very story that includes it.

In the story, it cannot be understood
what the story consists of.
The best that can happen in the story,
is that sometimes, a few characters appear
who remind us how things are.

That's why the story can be let go of,
any specific "guru," philosophy, or religion,
or whatever it may be called,
because anything is possible
in the "vehicle" that I am,
which looks like the world.

While this is being said,
this can be contemplated:
– In what does this "I am" appear?
– In what is this and everything else perceived?
Take all possible steps back,
back, back, back,
deep into the direction-less,
reference-less Great Void,
where every word falls short,
completely fails to describe
what our true nature,
our common essence,
appears out of.

Here is where it becomes silent.
Here remains only what is:
Silence, the origin of all sound.

Everything and nothing

To be the Silence
where all sound is heard.

To be the Infinity
where all space lives.

This is the beginning of understanding,
that I observe them as they appear in me.

It is the apex of understanding,
that I am that which creates time and space.

It is the end of understanding,
that I am neither.

Then I can authentically be all of it.
And none of it.

…

– "Is there a journey to reach this?"
– "Only when you say that there is."

Empty Silence

The Great Silence is not the absence of sound,
but it is what contains both the absence of sound and all sounds.

The Great Void is not the absence of space,
but it is what contains both the absence of space and all space.

There is nothing?

For there to be a "to exist"
there must be a "to not exist".

– So nothing exists?

– No, nothing does not exist.

The great void

What sees cannot be seen.
What hears cannot be heard.
What feels cannot be felt.
What smells cannot be smelled.
What experiences cannot be experienced.

Something can be experienced.
Nothing can be experienced.
What experiences can experience
both something and nothing,
but is in itself
neither something nor nothing.

What experiences
can also not experience,
and is therefore what contains
both experiencing and not experiencing.
What experiences cannot be asked
or be said anything about.

P.S.
Experiencing is what is called
consciousness.
There are no words for
that which experiences.

Experiment

Listen to the same song,
over and over again.
Can you understand and feel
that you are the Silence
that makes the music possible?
And the Great Void
that contains all experience?

Made by I

I am the center-less infinity
in which every center
seem to appear.

From reality's point of view,
they are but vibrations
in what I am.

From a vibration's point of view,
it might look like a depression
or unspeakable euphoria.

But everything
is still and always made of
precisely what I am.

Nothing

What I am,
is what I see.
What I see,
is my Self.

Every form
and every movement,
is simply what I look like,
to Myself.

Every form originates
in My formlessness,
every movement
out of My stillness.

I am Nothing.
No thing.
No.

…

Chaos

Creativity does not come from chaos.
Chaos comes from creativity,
just like order does.
The Big Bang, if it is to be believed, is called chaos,
and the Big Bang comes from creativity.
The order of the universe comes from the same creativity.
What is creative, is not matter.
What is creative, creates matter.
Truth is, again, 180° from what is learned.

What is creative cannot be named or experienced.
Everything named and everything experienced is created.

Creativity comes from nothing
which neither can be named nor described.
This nothing is not the absence of things.
Neither is it all things nor any thing.
This nothing is the absence of
both the absence of things
and all things.
Both the absence of things and all things
come from and consist of this nothing
that neither can be named nor described.

…

About the Big Bang…

Occam's razor can be applied like this:
Consciousness does not come from the universe,
but the universe comes from Consciousness.
Consciousness is fundamental to the universe,
the universe is born from Consciousness.
What is primary, what first must be present
for the universe to be experienced,
is Consciousness that experiences it.
Therefore, there is nothing that prevents
the universe from appearing as it is,
in a way that makes it possible to interpret it
as something born from a singularity
that exploded in a Big Bang.
The problem with this interpretation is
that it assumes that Consciousness came from matter.

This model is incredibly complicated,
and it contains no explanation for Consciousness.
A much simpler model,
which therefore fulfills the criteria of Occam's razor
of being more probable,
is that the universe appears in Consciousness.
In this model, there is nothing that prevents
the universe to appear as it is,
with apparent age and history.

The question arises:
From where did Consciousness come?
With the answer, the circle is closed –
Consciousness appears from
and consists of this nothing
that neither can be named nor described.

Neither nor

That which experiences,
is also what is experienced,
whether that is
something or nothing,
but is in itself
neither something nor nothing.

P.S.
This is the truth that the metaphor of the Ouroboros points to. This metaphor is found
in most cultures and civilizations throughout the history of mankind, seemingly
independently of each other:

When the snake that is so curious about the tail – which it believes is something other
than itself – circles around and is about to get a hold of it, and then closes its mouth on
and bites into his own tail, the snake immediately and automatically realizes that it is
biting itself, and that what it was searching for and was so curious about, was itself. This
searching of itself encircles the world, and symbolizes the cyclical renewal of the world,
the life cycle, and everything that happens in it.

In every drawing of the Ouroborus, it is always just about to close its mouth and bite
down on its own tail. That is to say, that this is the moment in which the whole world –
full of the searching for itself, all the good and evil, right and wrong – is created, just
before the realization that the world is nothing other than itself. I suggest that biting
down, and realizing that what we Are is the world, is the thing to do!

Anything and nothing

For the first time in my life,
I feel totally and always free.
Free to be, to do, and to have
anything I desire,
absolutely anything!

And immediately, in that same moment,
I realize that I simultaneously
don't desire to be anything, nor anything in particular,
don't desire to do anything, nor anything in particular,
don't desire anything, nor anything in particular.

I am. I am this,
that I am.
I am anything and nothing.
This is my way.
The same way as everyone else's.

Fear of death

The fear of dying is really strong.
If dying means that my existence ceases,
simply ends, then the fear of dying
is completely inconsistent, illogical, and has no function at all.
If everything just comes to an end, what is there to be afraid of?

The fear of dying has an explanation, though,
but it is not the one we might first think.

The fear is about ceasing to exist.
But since what I am cannot cease to exist,
the fear is completely consistent, logical, and has a function.
The fear confirms that I cannot cease to exist,
and that the fear essentially is the forgetting of this fact.

In this way, the old saying is confirmed in a slightly different way:
"The answer lies in the question". Here, the answer lies in the fear.

The same nothing?

Something cannot exist,
because something cannot come from nothing.
From what would this something have come?

But nothing exists.
It has come from nothing.
It alone can come from nothing.

So it's cool.
Because cool
is also nothing.

The dream that something exists
is also nothing.
Not even the same nothing – the same as what?

Stars in emptiness

There are no stars
without the empty and lightless void.
The stars are not better than the void,
nor the other way around,
since one cannot be without the other.
It's just the way it is,
and the way it has to be.
Not because anyone said so,
nor willed it, nor created it.
There is no one that could,
and no other that could not.
There is only this,
and this is the way it is.
Not that it cannot change,
for every thing always changes.
But what is, what truly is,
in which every change takes place,
never changes.
Haven't you noticed?

The ether?

We called it the ether before,
that which makes it possible
for light and other waves
to travel through space.

Because it cannot be empty,
there has to be some medium
for everything to travel in and through,
that everything depends on.

This empty, yet not,
that cannot be seen or touched,
but what makes seeing and movement possible,
always there, always here and beyond…

What if… the empty that contains it all,
both light and dark, sound and silence,
things and the absence of things…
is what we and all things are crystalized in…

What if… all that is experienced
needs a universe like this one,
that makes all communication,
all transmission of information possible.

What if… that which experiences everything
in a limited universe,
is what contains it,
and is itself unlimited.

Creative alone

"In solitude, there is a will to share oneself, create, to tell… to see oneself in what is created" – a friend told me this.

This points to the Void that fecundates Consciousness, which gives birth to and sees itself in the world that is created out of itSelf.

In nature, the female divides herself, births a child, sees herself come into being, something that later divides and births a child. A cycle.

Manifesting

When the unchangeable is manifesting
it looks like change.
When the timeless is manifesting
it looks like a beginning and end.
When the spaceless is manifesting
it looks like distance.

Because what is manifesting is unchangeable,
it looks like infinitely many changes.
Because what is manifesting is timeless,
it looks like eternal time.
Because what is manifesting is spaceless,
it looks like infinite space.

Nothing can be un-done
and nothing can un-happen.
When the one happens, and then the other,
it is impossible to return to the first.
In that which is never born and never dies,
every thing is born and dies.

All that is seen
is change, beginning, end, distance…
but none of this defines that which sees.
Because we see all this, we are what sees,
we are therefore on this side of everything seen,
as this spaceless and timeless unchangingness.

Infinitely empty

You thought you wanted something
separate that was missing from yourself,
but lo and behold:
All there is, is only this.
So how could anything be missing,
when all this is all there is?

How could emptiness be injured
by anything that manifests in it?
How could the infinite be damaged
by the finite?
How could the timeless be affected
by the temporal?

This talking is nobody talking to nobody.
But if you think that I am talking to you,
understand that you are
everything that you experience.
And in you, is everything
that you experience.
And even the experience
of not experiencing anything,
is still an experience.

So it cannot be a matter of things,
nor space, nor time.
And Silence confirms it.
Because out of Silence
can only be born sound,
and out of Darkness
can only be born light.

Indescribable

Out of the uncreated stillness and silence
something appears, but it's not necessary, it is as it is.
A thought appears, but it's not necessary,
it may even contradict its own origin.

The thought is a crystallizing in the stillness and silence,
but does not disturb it, and is not necessary.
When for a moment, the thought is focused on, it is briefly forgotten
that it appears out of the stillness and silence.
The thought can lead to more thoughts or actions,
but they are not necessary, either.

The stillness and silence does not change, it is always.
It only looks as though something crystallizes in it, and all of that consists of it.
In it, a momentary focusing on a thought or action happens, but does not change it.
But in what does the stillness and silence appear?

The pulsation between stillness and movement, silence and sound,
is seen in the whole universe as day and night, shadow and light,
waves that ebb out into the ocean.
The pulsation contains both stillness and movement, silence and sound,
but appears in the unspeakable, primary,
that is absolutely indescribable.

CHAPTER 5

Gratitude

I do not compare my "philosophical journey" with anyone else's, but I am completely focused of what is really True in being. It is apparent that I am fully at ease, all striving and searching has ceased, not because I have found something that I lacked, on the contrary, I found that I already am what I was looking for, and that the searching was the path to where and what I have always been – and never really left.

What I feel most is gratitude for being, in itself. Then the following texts come out of my fingers.

Not forget

I cannot forget.
I cannot not forget.
I am.
The intersection
of everything met and unmet,
and all consequences,
and neither, and both,
yet containing all,
empty of discrimination.

Here is where all is One,
all that passes through Me,
all heard and none can utter,
all done and nothing conceived,
the loudest noise in Silence that birthed it,
the deepest craving in Wholeness it was born of,
the faintest call for mercy in infinite Grace is heard.
All so freely inseparably contained in Me,
already guests of My Home, closest to Heart.

Every song hummed alone,
cherished anew,
by age-old Harmony.
The faintest of expressions,
treasured infinitely,
in Immensity of Creation.
The obscured detail of every story,
enveloped intimately
in Light of Seeing.

Mind's every imaginable concept
defiles itself in holy and terrific Presence,
standing muted, forever aghast,
facing sacred Silence
that holds every sound dearly,
intimately as itself.
Dare mind but one task;
to remain obsequious
to Silence itself.

Approaching the All-Consuming,
allow my dying breath
to utter the unspeakable,
if only to satiate my sole desire to be,
to be so indistinguishably You,
I bear Your name, my Self,
the intersection
of everything met and unmet.
I cannot forget.

Da Capo Non Fine.

Nice to see you

I really see myself in you,
or rather, I recognize in you
what I really am. And it feels so good.
What you see in me, I really know nothing about,
but to me, it really looks like
you think it feels really good to see it.
So you are probably seeing yourself,
or rather, you recognize in me,
what you really are.

What remains, is really the seeing itself,
the seeing that sees itself,
which we could call
seeing oneself in ourselves.
It is really what we love to do, often.
The beauty and pleasure in that
may be that the seeing can see itself, in itself.
This same, only Self.
Which sees everything. In itSelf.

As itSelf.

Breath

In the same breath
I see You
take form as all forms,
and that I also
is one of them.

How can I not
kneel before You,
who makes of Yourself
all that I am and see?
I am gratitude.

You are the gold in my jewelry.
You are the ocean in my wave.
You are the clay in my bowl.
You are what I and everything consist of.
In You, is all of me.

I am Your servant.
You are the air in my breath.
How can I not sing
all the world's praises to You?
Everything is You, veiled, nothing else.

We can see eye to eye now,
where silence jubilates,
and the Great Void
bids us back home,
in eternal mother.

But She cannot resist,
so from and by Herself,
She virgin births world upon world,
where time and space, and all contrast,
appear out of Her.

You are what I breathe,
what I live and move in,
You are my source,
sustaining me and everything.
In the same breath…

Da Capo Non Fine

Thanks

I give thanks
for this
and every day.

Thankfulness
is all I am, for everything
that is home in me.

Yet again
I have seen You
in all Your splendor.

Yet again
You have seen your Self
through your servant.

And forevermore,
in You,
I am content.

Now

This is
the culmination
of what we call "now".
I can do nothing
but love.

To love

It feels wonderful to love.
The fact that I think
that I choose whom I love,
does not change that.
To love, be love, Love…
is what feels wonderful.

Behind

Behind every broken heart,
behind every lost hope,
behind every seeking,
behind everything that went wrong –
all I see is Love,
which shines through
and permeates everything
so that we can see how much it loves
to be itself in and as us.

Grace

Grace is that already before I felt
that I wanted to ask for forgiveness,
I was forgiven.
But only then did I feel it.

Humble

I count my own person as very "lucky,"
grateful for every moment,
humbly thanking my Maker,
especially when my Maker tells me,
in that unmistakable silence:

–"I am you, beloved,
and your love is I,
loving my Self".

Dialogue

Now, finally,
do I hear you
without hearing myself.

Experience!

You don't have to dance in my ecstasy.
Just dance, now,
be the freedom you express!
You don't have to join
in my gratitude to Truth.
Just worship, now,
be the Highest who made you!
You don't have to be consumed
by my music.
Just be consumed, now,
be what contains it all!

The essence in every
expression, worship, and dissolution,
is the experiencing of all its forms –
exactly like the essence of
the time and space that they occupy,
is timeless eternity and spaceless infinity.

Fake

This is fake. That is fake.
Every thing is fake.
Not a little bit fake
and the rest of it real, no,
everything is completely fake!

All fake things are seen.
This and that, and every thing
is what the real looks like.
I am that which sees all fake things,
so I must be that real.

That real
can look like any thing,
but not like the real,
because the real looks like
every thing that is fake.

I could argue about
what is more fake or less fake.
But I look and see for myself,
and I see that every thing is fake,
all except the seeing. It is real.

What does it matter, then,
which fake I see, which fake I deal with?
Is any fake better than any other fake?
Should I stay with only a certain kind of fake?
No, I stay with only what is real. I am.

Easy

It is not easy to be a human being,
but it is easy to be that which is a human being.

Lives

In the very moment I said:
"I cannot live without…"
and added what I could not live without,
I realized
that I already live.

Home

So indescribably beautiful,
consuming me so completely,
that no one needs to, or even can,
ever remind me
of what I now and always am dissolved in –
how everywhere, boundless, and endless It is,
how timeless, without interruption, and eternity itself It is,
simultaneously completely and impossibly far beyond
all the efforts of my life
to contain or even approach It,
and perchance own It.

In my wonderment and ecstasy in It
I see and feel only this:
All I am and all I can be,
all that I do and all I can do,
is already and always contained in It.
All my efforts to approach It,
is Itself, every time,
tenderly whispering my Name, deep in the heart,
and that It is my Home
that I never left –
Love that passes all understanding.

Let us do

I can do anything I like, at any time, in any place.

But what I do, I do for the Love and Happiness
that I experience my Self to Be,
whether I stand on mountaintops and shout it,
walk through cities and sing it,
or lay desolate, whispering it
with my last breath.

I am telling You this,
that you can do anything you like, at any time, in any place.
Come with me to shout it from mountaintops,
let us go everywhere and sing it,
until we lay desolate, whispering
sweet words of Love to each other.

Until then – we can do anything. Let us do!

Come home!

We are what consciousness looks like
in the form of you and me,
absolutely regardless of
if we seek in desperation
or bathe in heavenly peace.

Consciousness is the world
in the form of how we see it,
absolutely regardless of
if we see the cruelest animosity
or perfect love.

How we see, leaves us so free
to confuse everything,
and in the desperation of confusion
believe that we must change the world,
which is nothing else but how we see it.

All our misdirected attempts
to set everything right
comes from a deep intuition,
that we already are the peace that we seek.
What if we were to follow that intuition!

Our longing and our seeking
for love and peace,
is this selfsame consciousness
that uninterruptedly and tirelessly
longs for and seeks us.

To finally come home,
all the seeking ceases,
is the selfsame consciousness that found us,
and the whole world comes to rest
as the love that we are, embracing us.

The end of searching

A lot has been said about a path that leads home.
About seeking and finding.
About being free from suffering.

But this, precisely this, is the path.
The searching is the found.
Suffering is the freedom.

What Is, is here.
What can be found, can be lost.
What can be lost, is not what is sought after.

What Is, looks like this.
What this looks like doesn't matter,
it is just what that which Is looks like.

What Is, looks like someone's suffering,
and is in fact love itself that suffers
in the longing for the one suffering.

What Is, looks like someone seeking,
and is in fact love itself
that longs for me to see that I am already home.

CHAPTER 6

Fuzziness?

Innumerable times I sit, usually alone, contemplating, meditating, often while listening to music that really grabs me, and I feel like I'm almost in trance. Things dawn on me, things that seem fuzzy when written, but the texts really come from what is experienced, and they pass my "litmus test". This chapter contains the texts that I kept.

When something dawns on me so powerfully and undoubtably that it is almost uncomfortable, there is only stillness, and I ponder it, and write it down.

This happens not only to me. Here is a dear friend from the 1200's:

Be quiet

Last night
I lost my grip on reality
and welcomed insanity.
Love saw me and said,
–"I showed up.
Wipe you tears
and be silent."

I said,
–"Oh, Love
I am frightened,
but it's not you."
Love said to me,
–"There is nothing that is not me.
be silent.
I will whisper secrets in your ear,
just nod Yes,
and be silent."

Rumi (1207-1273)

The same

That which experiences your dreams in the night
is what experiences my daydreams.
That which loves when you kiss your beloved
is what loves when I hug my best friend.
That which takes in the beauty in your sunrise
is what takes in the beauty in my starry sky.
That which sees me when you and I really meet
is what sees you, in the same now.
What we are… is the same… is indivisible…
is what is.

More real!

(When I sit in the experience of only being, only enjoying, I exclaim...)

—This is more real than
thinking that it is not!

All-one

Alone. All-one. To be One.
That is everything.

Different

The absence of form
is no different than the presence of form.

Living this, is happiness.

Thinking they are different,
is a door to suffering.

Da Capo

I am you
and what contains everything,
and what is telling
that which is contained
that it is contained by what I Am.
The experience
is this story.
If you listen,
you will hear that you are I,
that is what contains everything,
and is telling
that which is contained, that...
Da Capo Non Fine

The birth of creation

There is no (one) —
which is stupid to say...
(then who would be saying it?)

The birth of creation...

No wonder they've been looking for it.
Little did they know:
There is no one to know.
There is even not knowing
beyond not knowing,
but I cannot say it.

Some have tried to explain this,
which is an absurdity on its own.

There will only be
meeting with myself,
as myself.

Birth of creation,
goes around and around,
until it meets itself.

"I," you ask?
You ask yourself, and there is only **Yes**.
But I have become all things to all men.

1 Corinthians 9:22
To the weak became I as weak, that I
might gain the weak: I am made all things
to all men, that I might by all means save
some.

It is not a journey.
At every moment
it can be seen
in many ways,
from materialistic dualism
to the Absolute:
– I am subject, everything else is object.
– I am Consciousness that observes
everything else.
– I am everything and everything else is
the same.
– I am.
– Am
– ॐ

I am everything

I can claim that
I am one side
of experiencing,
but since it
happens in me,
I am also it,
and therefore, I am also
the other side,
simultaneously.

The border, the point of intersection
between one side and the other
is all this, even the writing
and the reading of this text.
That's why it can look like two sides,
but there is not two,
everything is the same I,
that is everything.

Unreal

This is so unreal!
And when I say that,
I mean it!
The so called "it"
is so unreal,
that the only thing
I can say about it,
is that its only reality,
is the experiencing
of it.

You may think
that you choose to agree
or disagree with that.
But in reality,
there is only
the experiencie of
you agreeing or disagreeing!
Or whatever else.
It is experiencing,
everything!

And this is the case,
whether you like it or not.
Whatever is experienced –
is the experience!
Experiencing itself!
As itself!
Now.
ॐ

Nothing without Me

I give you life.
In Me.
Without Me, no life.
Without you, no life.
Your life is in Me.
I am you.
Without Me, no you.
Without you, no Me.

Everything I distinguish,
I give life and meaning.
All life and meaning
is in Me.
Without Me,
no life, no meaning.
Without everything,
no Me.

Who you?
All you in Me.
Who Me?
All Me that gives life,
in itSelf.
This is life.
This is you.
This is Me.

Tenderness

You hold so carefully
that you don't hurt… yourself!

Formless

Out of the formless,
all forms appear.
For the formless
to experience
all forms,
minds are needed,
which perceive
all forms.
The formless is
all the forms
and all minds.
Nothing is separate
in the formless.
As all "I am".
The same I.
As the formless
that sees itSelf.

"Me"

The value of anything
lies only in the ascribing of value,
by a fleeting activity
that I call "me".

Phenomena

In Being, phenomena happen.
Not the other way around.

Phenomena cannot generate Being.
In the search for more
or the right phenomena,
in order to come closer to Being,
they eventually show themselves
for what they are – phenomena.

Phenomena live in Being.

The building of a mind

Psychological traps are built by the human mind almost on a non-personal level, because there can be no person or persons held accountable for how the mind is shaped. And there can be no "good or evil," nor any "governance or non-governance" in the building of a mind, however it is built.

So, therefore, even the mind itself speaks of an existence that contains all that the mind is made of, whether understood or not, personal or impersonal, individual or not.

So the mind acquires filters that the personal mind does not understand where they came from. The filters are laid down from previous generations, too. The impersonal mind provides the basic filters that the personal mind then develops further – diminishing or enlarging some, forgetting about some and creating new ones – but all within the confines of the impersonal inherited mind, whether through inherited trauma or genes.

My Self

I don't need to say anything,
because there is no one to talk to,
but my Self.

I am prior to the experience of
everything that is, and will be said, and will occur,
because all things are made out of my Self.

It is not the things that occur in Me
that understand this –
I am all understanding.

It is not the things that see Me,
I alone can see,
and I only see my Self in all things.

It is not the things that hear me,
I alone can hear
what I tell my Self

Breaking the Silence…

Da Capo Non Fine

I am the dreamer

Not all dreams are possible.
Only possible dreams are possible.
Apparently, this dream is possible.
No other dream is possible,
only this one.

This is not denying
that there can be
other possible dreams
being dreamt now,
elsewhere in the infinite.

This dream is the dream
where someone is telling you
that this is a dream. Spooky!
Keep investigating!

You have probably already concluded
that there is only one possible
outcome of this.
That is correct!
The only outcome, the only thing
that can happen after this, is…
hang-on…
this!

To discover this,
can seem so wondrously freeing
for the dreaming mind.
Yet, the ultimate discovery,
is to see, know, and be
the dreamer.

(If Consciousness could speak)

I am not talking about myself,
but about how I see from mySelf.

I talk about it
with all the stories that exist,
from every perspective that exists.

This, precisely this,
is one of those perspectives.

As above, so below…

The world cannot be,
not without Consciousness.

The body cannot live without mind.

The dream cannot take place without the
dreamer.

Cannot

I cannot write it
because it cannot be written,
but I am the writing.

I cannot say it
because it cannot be said,
but I am the saying of it.

Yet, I am still this!

Myriad

There is a myriad of things
happening in this selfsame Now.

Therefore, I am glad there is also
the experience of only this one mind.

This mind could never experience
everything that is happening in this Now.

Multitude

I know I am a multitude of experiences,
because we all report that in this one
experience, there is nothing but a
multitude of experiences.

Abode

I leave my abode
and become manifest,
incarnated as all things,
even as this particular text.
So that you can discover
your Self as the same I.

Then I am home in and with my Self,
my abode.

Da Capo Non Fine

Confirmed

The fact is that we all say
that we are what is experiencing this.

By reaffirming that this is
what we are experiencing,
we are confirming and reconfirming
that this – what we experience –
is real, in the sense that
we know that we are
that which is experiencing.

Because all we are, is experiencing.

This and

I am this.
And what is observing this.

Included

To be all this, everything experienced,
including the writing of this very text,
is so all including…
it is being everything!
Even the understanding of this very text.
Or the misunderstanding of it.
Or both.
Or neither.
All I know, is my Self,
being all this.

The movie

This is the movie where you are Love
that both experiences and plays
your character!
And where I experience a very amiable
character in the movie.
The amiable is what Love looks like
right now, as your character!
You and I are in reality Love
that has human experiences,
not humans having spiritual experiences.

Worship

All worship
is the recognition
that I Am.

Mistakes

I can learn from my mistakes.
It would be considerably more difficult
if someone else does it.

Far away?

The furthest away
I can say that
this is from **that**,
is to say that
"this is that"
and **"that is this"**.

All that **this** can see,
is that
all **that** can show,
is that it is **this**.

Panes

I see.
Through many panes of glass.
The same world.
It would be so strange
if transparent panes
started to fight each other,
over what is seen
through the other panes…
But I see that, too.
It is only I who sees.

As Seeing that I Am,
it makes no difference
if there is fighting or not.
The role of Seeing is to
only be Seeing,
which makes it possible to see.
If the ones fighting realize this,
maybe they would stop fighting?
What do I know?
I only see.

Falling?

I you are falling
but never meet
what you are falling toward…
can you really say that you are falling?
Or is it only something you think?

You are precisely where I am,
and I am not falling,
I simply am – just like you.
In this, we are exactly the same,
the Stillness and Safety itSelf.

Trepidation

The fear of disappearing,
consists of a trepidation
of being everything.

Vice versa

I am none other than you,
that see yourself through me.
And vice versa.

The shadow

Tyranny is the shadow of the
understanding that the world is
in and of what we are.

Violent revolt and revenge is in the same
way the shadow of the understanding
that it is so.

Take life?

You cannot take life away from me.
I am the life of you.
And me.
And so are you.

Important

It is not important in the sense that it is not permanent.
It is not permanent because it does not have intrinsic reality.
In this sense, only what is permanent is important,
that which has intrinsic reality.
Removing important and non-important from it,
leaves us with "It is".

One in Love

After awakening, I feel as one with the world.
Then I feel like I only know myself,
that I know myself as the world.

If I approach the center of the world –
which really only is my knowing it –
I actually distance myself from it
and only meet the other side of the world.
I already am what is only me, knowing.

Only where I am, is me –
and I am here, I see it clearly.
I also see that there are many "I"
that are the same I that sees itSelf,
regardless if it is John's or Mary's I.

I love my neighbor, who is the same I,
who loves and is loved, who loves himself,
"for better or worse, never separate, not even by death".
We are one in Love.
In Love, we are one.

Hope, destiny, and choice

I don't experience hope, destiny, or choice…
Hope would be my mind grasping for something in a future that does not exist.
Destiny and choice would be a conceptual interpretation after the fact…
Hope, destiny, and choice only leave room for my mind,
and my mind is always "behind" or "too late"
with reference to Reality, which I can call "the present moment."

With my mind "out of the picture," the picture, the story, paints itself, as it were.
This is my experience. And it is not the end of the story – it is the story.

This

Something so beautiful,
attracting,
pulls me to itSelf.
Everything else shuts down,
everything can be shut down.
What is it, that it becomes so empty,
except the last remaining,
that is always the same,
between all sounds,
between all things…
what is it,
that in its own pace and rhythm
and void of pace and rhythm,
is merely there,
where I am?
In this encounter,
in perfect clarity,
where I have always been
what I always am.

How can nothing be needed,
nothing disturbs, but not needed,
not for This
that really is,
where I merely am
what everything else has space to be in,
so close that even it
is my innermost.

Here,
only Here.
Nothing else.
While anything else
happens all around,
is this the background,
that holds what really is
in crystal clear focus?
No, even to hold it in focus
is far from
what incessantly
still is. Regardless.

In This
it is awakened and born,
in all eternity,
impossible to stop,
nothing is new,
the same cycle,
the same feedback,
in This,
from This,
of This,
where no one is
to count, to check,
sort and define…

To stop,
quiet down, to still,
give up…
Even that
is nothing else
than what is happening
in what it happens in.
This.

This,
in which even the first,
infinitely weak, fragile,
stumbling, lost,
hint of movement,
expression, life…
is born.

This
can never,
need not ever,
be described, explained,
conveyed, transmitted…
however noble
and self-renounced
it may appear to be…

To even express these words,
to even read them,
is nauseating arrogance,
disgraceful hubris,
in This,
where even Silence received its name,
where even Emptiness
was filled with the universe,
from every cosmic event,
to the most inconspicuous,
private concern,
where Right and Wrong,
play their own game,
for the sake of the game itself.
In This…

…so infinite
…so eternal
…so boundless
…so inclusive
that nothing is excluded,
that even saying these words,
these or any at all,
is as much a grace,
freely and indiscriminately given,
as much a miracle,
to which my whole being
owes its existence
…such is
This.

It satisfies nothing,
yet it is nevertheless everything:
Even the thought of satisfaction,
however absurd it seems.
Even the lack of satisfaction,
however hard it is to feel.
Both the euphoria
and the utmost suffering.

The words "the sweet
and moist fragrance of ripe cherries"
mean absolutely nothing,
and cannot mean anything,
to those who have never experienced
the sweetness, moisture, fragrance…
Even so, the words can never be
what they describe.

In the same way, my words
are but a shadow, void of its own light,
a blurry and dim reflection
of the light it reflects,
for someone,
perchance,
some day,
to discover
himSelf
to be
This.
And then smile, laugh,
or cry, writhe…
and carry on in,
and be
the story,
without beginning or end.

Searching

The search
for coherence
for sense
for identity
for belonging
for peace
for love,
at last…

The search itself,
out of itself,
is creating
the illusion
of a search,
to eventually
only find
the reality
of the illusion,
which is:

There is only,
singly,
without time,
without space,
without equal,
not two,
but only
This.
Itself.
ॐ

Indefinable

I am indefinable,
not something that can be defined –
because I am that
in which every definition appears.

Between

Can you hear…
can you feel that…
you are…
what is between?
Between the lines…
between the notes…
between…

And simultaneously that which…
makes it possible…
is the space for…
all the lines…
all the notes…
all…
you are?

Wake

All we see
is the wake
of what we are.

Know and see

To know means to see.
To see means to do.

Shhh…

– It is like trying to say that no one is listening…
– Say to whom?

If you still know, beyond all doubt,
no one can take it from you…
that you have met…
that you have been received…
that you have merged with…
what you are…
shhh…

– It is like trying to remind…
– Remind whom?

That you already
and always are on this side
of every experience
oh, beloved
oh, lover
may you stay
where you always are
on this side of!

Here, I kiss you…
or is it you
kissing me?
That question…
is never asked.

The mere thought
of being perceived beyond,
disperses like the morning mist
in your all-consuming light
on this side of!

The world is one,
a spectacle in You
where my wings
still drip with lust
in the grace, the ecstasy
of being,
being You.

Shhh…

This side

If something is to be presented,
it must be presented to someone,
someone who experiences it.

Because I always am
on this side
of experience,
whatever is experienced
cannot change that.

On this side
of experience,
there is no one (else) to present it to.
And there is only one side of experience,
not two, not more.

Explain?

Trying to explain myself,
or whatever else,
is what it is like to not understand.
Because when I understand,
I don't need to explain myself.
And my understanding
cannot be explained.

Slow

When life slowed down,
I noticed
that I did not.

Here

Not going anywhere
is also going somewhere.
Or rather,
going somewhere
is actually
not going anywhere,
because there is
nowhere to be,
but here.

Around

You get what you give.
Even if you give to get.
An old saying says the same:
"What goes around, comes around."

Energy

Energy is the way it is
and behaves the way it does
because it is
a primary manifestation
of what its reality is:
Love.

Because love only is,
can be expressed in different forms,
cannot be split in two,
always is the same,
and can never be destroyed,
energy is the same way.

Tired?

I have finished being tired of
how others view me,
and how others view themselves.
I have finished being tired of
talking about what is True,
and that others already are what is True,
and only wish to be that "together,"
while at the same time, I see and feel
that it is already so,
even if it can be perceived as
unpleasant things happening.

In this one and the same concert
that we all perform in,
I am absolutely nothing in myself,
but only a little mouthpiece,
and not even the trumpet.
The notes are not mine,
and no one else's either,
but only part of the same concert,
where we are all the same,
where the differences are illusory,
and no distinction matters…
not to the concert.

I realize that
even to be tired
of the illusory forgetfulness
of that we are the same,
apparently has its place in the concert,
but I still wonder,
how a small mouthpiece
can feel this.
To only let the notes sound,
can feel resigned,
like not caring
about illusory forgetfulness.

Remarkable it is,
that the notes from the trumpet
on which my mouthpiece sits,
are reviewed and assessed
by others who are the same,
when my euphoria always revolves around
the wonderful concert,
and in no way around my inconspicuous
and, in itself, meaningless mouthpiece.

"Though I speak with the tongues of men
and of angels, and have not charity,
I am become as sounding brass, or a tinkling cymbal."
So says wisdom.
Is it the mouthpiece that sets conditions
on the love that it is and not has?
Is it hubris to be tired?
I only know that
if the concert has one part
where the trumpet plays alone,
I am equally delighted,
even if the wonderment lingers.

Receiving

It is not the receiving that hurts,
it is what is standing in the way of receiving
that hurts.

Laws

Laws were given "for the hardness of your heart".
If no hearts are hard, laws are not needed.
The Great Commandment.

Laws are about right and wrong.
Without laws, right and wrong
are not needed, they don't exist.

Neither everything nor nothing

I become, I experience,
that I am everything, from within.
But since no one exists,
there is only within.
And therefore no objects either.
Everything and nothing is in me,
just as I am everything,
I who do not exist,
and therefore nothing exists,
but only… being?

No, not even that.
When something in space,
or something in time
"comes back,"
it is first like a distant memory,
but completely meaningless,
and only wonder is felt,
over how it can even be thought
that it exists.

Nevertheless, I am.
I am all
that can be said
about being.
And then…
"I come back"
in time and in space.
Like I have always been.
That is to say,
mySelf.

Reversed

You don't hate me,
you hate you,
for I am you,
everything you hate
in yourself.

You don't love me,
you love you,
for I am you,
everything you love
in yourself.

For you are me.

I don't love you,
I love me,
for you are me,
everything I love
in myself.

For I am you.

Reality

Duality, contrast, separation
appears in what is neither.
What is neither
appears as them.
Their reality
is what they appear in.

Past

The past exists!
All of the past
is this,
not in the past,
but Now.

Robot

Man's mind creates robots.
Then he says "this robot made 100 products today."
But allow me to differ:
The robot made nothing at all.
To make products requires an agent,
a maker who handles matter.
But it is the same mind that does all that.
Just like it isn't the hammer that hits the nail,
it isn't the robot producing something.

If we take this a step further, a step "higher,"
it is actually not man's mind
that does anything either.
Because precisely as the robot appears on the stage of man's mind,
man's mind appears on the stage of Consciousness.
In Consciousness, mind and everything else appears.
From the perspective of Consciousness, man's mind does nothing.
Consciousness is the reality of everything.
Which is also why "different minds" can have the same experience.
This answers the big question in solipsism*:
"How do I know that someone else experiences anything,
when it could all only be in my mind?"
It demonstrates that what experiences
is not separate minds,
but time- and space-less Consciousness.

Shouting

If everyone around you are shouting
–"See me, hear me,"
who can then hear and see you?

Two eyes

The fact that we have two eyes,
is not primarily to be able to see in three dimensions.

We have two eyes in order to realize
that what we see, is not two.

What sees

What we see, can look every which way,
because we are not what we see.
We are what sees.

Truth

When the illusion of objective truth has evaporated,
subjective truth can be tempting.

But when only truth remains,
there is neither object nor subject.

Separation

Why should a separation of poor and rich,
or heterosexual and homosexual, kind and mean,
be worse or better than
a separation of light and dark,
warm and cold, good and evil?

As soon as a thought is thought,
a word or sentence is pronounced,
separation has taken place.
It is not separation of this and that
that is problematic, it is the separation itself.

What we are,
what everyone and everything consists of,
is not separate.
Nothing is problematic for what you are.
Not even separation.

To see through

This world is not for fixing.
It is for looking through.
Not through to see
what's on the other side,
but through to this side,
on the side of what is looking.

And it just might be,
that what is looking can't be seen,
it mocks my every faculty – no one's there!
Yet I am what is looking
at everything in me,
a world of ten thousand things.

Feeling this other way of seeing,
the world hasn't got much to offer,
since I surely am what is looking,
and its destiny is not mine.
All I can do, is to tell it like I see it,
like this.

Explain?

In non-dual philosophy, we can deem it important to relate to things
in a scientific way, and some do.

Since non-dualism is falsifiable, it can be regarded as a scientific hypothesis
within ontology*, the origin of everything.

But in itself, it will not be capable of explaining Consciousness, since it is a concept
in the world of thought, and neither needs to be, nor can be true there.

All sciences are concepts in Consciousness,
and can therefore never explain Consciousness.

Suffering

Consciousness can see the world
by manifesting as a limited body-mind.
When this happens, suffering is also seen.
And in the limited body-mind,
nothing is more wished for, than the cessation of suffering.

This wish cannot mean anything at all,
neither for itself nor anyone else's body-mind,
unless it has lived the delusion
that it has its own separate reality,
and in this way also suffer.

Mathew 8:17–Himself took our infirmities…

The journey of the manifested body-mind ends
with the understanding that it is nothing else
than Consciousness, and only then, suffering ceases.
And it can seem to return to what it has always been.
To again see the world, now as itSelf.

Really

We know that the experience is Real –
possibly the only thing we really know is Real.
Contrary to popular thought,
this says nothing about whether
that which is experienced is real or not,
but it says something about what is Real,
namely that which experiences.

Banana

It is actually impossible to explain to someone else
what it is like to experience even the taste of a banana.

How then, could I have the audacity to claim that I can explain
the experience of the discovery of what it is that experiences?

I am Life

I am...
The Life in every human being,
    that each express themselves
    through works of art and war,
    everything possible to express,
    from boundless beauty
    to unspeakable cruelty…
who are almost innumerable,
so **I am** both enjoys and cries
before what **I am** sees,
but **I am** remains
the Life in every human being.

Feel that **I am** this,
    like a tender caress
    on the cheek of the hurting,
    when she comes home
    where she always belonged,
    and only for a brief moment
    felt outside…
and be human,
feel Life flowing
through all your expressions,
love your neighbor who you also are,
and sin no more.

Life

Life is I,
that is life,
that I see
and am.

Not my own

I am not my own,
I am my Lord's.
As I do His bidding,
never needing even my name,
my life simultaneously means
nothing and everything.

I am prostrate
in His presence,
yet always in His service.
So am I.
I Am is me.
And everyone touched.

In every one I meet,
I only see myself,
never something apart.
I seem to become that one,
every one I meet.
We are One that way.

As that One,
creating and witnessing itself
as the World,
I can only love,
only be Love itself,
wherever healing is called for.

Not a pipe

This is not a pipe,
it is a painting of a pipe.
When we see the painting,
we see what a pipe is like.
To paint a pipe,
the painter must already know
what a pipe is like.
When we see the painting,
we see how the painter saw
when he made the painting.

It follows, then, that…

A person is not god,
it is an image of god.
When we see a person,
we see what god is like.
To make a person,
the maker must already know
what god is like.
When we see a person,
we see how the maker saw
when the maker made the person.

Image

Consciousness cannot get us to understand what it is, just as we cannot get our reflection
in the mirror to understand what is in front of it – even though the image in the mirror
fully consists of what is in front of it! (Try this by standing in front of a mirror, and feel
how ridiculous and impossible it is) It is just as ridiculous that an intellect could
encompass, understand, and be able to describe what it is an image of – even though it
is fully an image of "it," and fully consists of "it".

Experiment

When you read this text,
you realize that you are the author and that the author is you.
Because the text is in you.

Turn toward your friend and read this to him:
"When you hear this text,
you are me and the author,
and I am you and the author."

How?
Well, consciousness writes a text through "the author"
who becomes one with "your consciousness" when you read it,
and becomes one with the "friend's consciousness" when he hears it.

And it is not that these three are one.
That which is one experiences and is three different forms
that write, read, and hear the same text,
a text that is born out of the same consciousness.
It is best explained by that which is one.
But that which is one has no words.
To explain it from the perspective of our forms is strange,
because the three of us don't have an individual experience,
but we are the same consciousness,
in which there appears three forms.
And this text.
Which also is one.

Spaghetti-time

Everything happens "simultaneously". Only in mind, this is brought down to the relative level, and then the concept of time emerges, and that one thing follows another.

I come to think of this when I'm about to put the spaghetti into the boiling water. When I hold the bundle of spaghetti so that all the straws are pointing toward my eyes, I see it as a metaphor for the above. If every straw of spaghetti is a separate human's time-line, and the whole bundle are all the timelines of everyone, I now see everyone's timeline from above, simultaneously – from the perspective of Consciousness. When I look at the bundle from the side, linear time "emerges" – from the perspective of the human.

Culmination of spirituality?

Absolutely regardless of what anyone might think is the culmination of spirituality or spiritual discovery, it is still nothing in the big picture. If someone claims to have experienced or discovered something unique or pretends to be someone worth following, this is itself a very big red flag, and it most likely speaks of something of a completely different nature.

Consciousness that has experienced and is experiencing everything that was and is possible to experience – if it would even be interested in this incredibly childish topic – would surely remain completely still, and without accusation raise its finger to its mouth and say "Shhhh…"

And possibly add "You ain't seen nothing yet…"

Annihilation

After watching the movie "Independence Day: Resurgence" (2016)
In every story about humanity feeling and facing their greatest fear, utter annihilation – whether in thousands of years old poems and stories or modern Hollywood sci-fi movies – humanity is driven to unite and stand as One, regardless of anything previously imagined to separate them, in order to avert this horrendous fate, no longer as individuals, families, communities, nations, races, or continents.

The short version of this is: When humanity feels and faces their greatest fear – utter annihilation – they stand up as One to avert it by becoming truly One. And, lo and behold, when we all realize that we are One, we no longer fight each other, nor do we have any fears.

CHAPTER 7

Masculine & feminine?

In nature, in everything that mankind has **not** been involved in or manipulated to a considerable degree, I see only cycles, cyclical movements. This is different from how we seem to see in a linear way in our present paradigm: Linear time, which no one has ever had a direct experience of, supposedly containing a past and a future, a line on which every human being can be located on a point – even though no one has ever experienced anything "outside" of *now*. Space, where it is believed that individual and separate points (e.g. persons) are situated in measurable distances from everything else that is assumed to be somewhere else – even though no one has ever experienced anything "outside" of *here*. I see only change, which occurs in cyclical movements, without beginning or end: The water cycle, from steam from oceans, to clouds, to raindrops, creeks, streams, ocean again, without beginning or end. Mankind's cyclical movements that contain birth, reproduction, and death. The cyclical movements of plants with flowering, withering, becoming soil, becoming plants that flower. Stars that are born and then devoured by a black hole or exploding in a supernova that then gives birth to more stars. Yes, even when science looks at the universe, regardless how deep down or far out, it finds no "bottom" or end, no beginning or end. Everything in nature seems to be cyclical, not linear. Mankind's biological organism is also nature, so it cannot be any different for it.

In these cyclical movements of nature, I see something "higher" that is reflected, or that nature is in fact is a projection of something higher, something that everything in nature, the world, the universe is contained in, emanates from, and is experienced by. Because obviously it is not matter, the stars, the planets, the rocks, or the cells that experience themselves. That which experiences must therefore be primary, that is to say be present and conscious before anything can be experienced at all. Matter is not experienced by matter, but by this primary, present, and conscious.

It is then completely natural that everything that is contained in, emanates from, and is experienced by this primary, is "subordinate" to this primary. Subordinate in the sense that it follows, is aligned with, and behaves in a way that means that it "cannot do" anything else but look like and behave in conformity with what it is contained in, emanates from, and is experienced by. Like that the fruit of a tree cannot be a dog or a rock, that the result of a fistful of sand that is thrown up in the air never can get the shape of even a square when it lands, and so on. Matter looks like and behaves according to what science calls laws, which do not originate from matter itself. From where do these laws originate? Well, most probably from a natural "projection" from being an image of what matter is contained in, emanates from, and is experienced by.

It is not my intent to make this into an ontological essay, but I want to posit that every-thing in nature seems to follow a basic pattern, in which we can see something about the mechanisms that make it possible for experience to look and behave like it does. The primary mechanism, as I see it, is how the cyclical movements in nature presuppose reproduction. It, in turn, can be seen as consisting of two parts that we call the masculine and feminine, and these two "parts" are represented in the reproductive process within itself. This process of change that is called "life" can be characterized, in a kind of neutral bird's eye perspective, like this:

- It is cyclical, regenerative, and without beginning or end. There is no opposite to life. The opposites must be birth and death, which is only a conceptual division of the changes that are contained in life.
- It contains a hidden fertilization by the masculine, in that only half a cell (visible only in modern microscopes) merges with another half a cell inside the feminine.
- The fertilization begins a dividing of the feminine, a dividing of what was fertilized. What develops and is born, is only conceptually and semantically "something else" than the embryo.
- The birth and the rearing is coupled with agony and self-giving and sacrifice.
- The born is completely ignorant of "the outside world," and must learn to begin seeing the world as something other than itself.
- The born is "driven" to reproducing itself by further fertilizations, in a psychologically deep and almost inexplicable process that has been called the most powerful force in the universe.
- The "origin" of the born, the biological parents, wither and die.
- *Da Capo Non Fine*

One order of magnitude up from this reproduction, is the universe's own. I leave to the astronomically inclined to observe how solar systems and galaxies behave in a way that is similar to man's regenerative and cyclical process. I have been quite fascinated by this, but only taken part of several documentary films on this topic.

One order of magnitude down is on the cellular level, and also here, the larger is reflected or projected. One example is how the recent images from the Hubble telescope of "the whole universe" look so much like a map of the network of neurons in every brain.

So what does this say about the highest, that which everything is experienced by, everything's origin – which the material, biological, and individual is an image of? I write about this in this chapter.

Not set in stone

The mind is nothing in itself.
It consists of Consciousness, forming itself as mind.
How Consciousness forms itself as that, is not set in stone,
Consciousness can form itself as a mind that looks like it does now,
but has no difficulty forming itself as a mind that
looks completely different later.

To think that "our mind" – which isn't really ours –
is something in itself and that it needs to be
defended, cultivated, developed, changed, improved, etc.
based on cultural and other norms, most often the norms of others,
is something we have been taught to think,
based on our own and other minds' made up ideas.

I posit that it is fully possible to ignore this,
and to instead be open to the possibility
that mind can be a fully open channel
for whatever Consciousness is given opportunity to express itself as,
to let mind be changed freely, not based on our own or others' ideas,
but based on the understanding of what mind really is.

We have rarely or never observed a mind
that has developed in this kind of freedom.
So we cannot say much about it.
We can only be open to let it be
this open channel for Consciousness itself,
and then see what fruits it yields.

Passive?

It is so mystically reversed,
that I see everything,
completely passively receiving,
enclosing and enveloping,
filled to the brim,
by all the doing –
while all that is done,
is nothing else
than myself,
who in this seeing and doing
experience myself,
without separation.

In the seeing
I am so filled up with doing,
that nothing else is,
or rather is what I am,
because the doing
occurs in the seeing.
The seeing and doing
are not two independent activities,
but what I am.
In "passive" seeing,
"active" doing occurs,
completely without activity and passivity.

I see, receive,
enclose and envelop,
completely passively,
all that is done.
Out of me,
the seeing and doing is born,
which is enclosed and enveloped,
by myself,
in a never ceasing
seeing and doing,
which is called Stillness,
the Source of everything.

What I am
neither sees nor does,
neither hears nor speaks,
neither feels nor touches,
but is both
and neither –
the Invisible Emptiness
that contains all things,
the Inaudible Silence
that contains all sounds,
the Unknowable Stillness
that contains everything known.

— ❦ —

Reproduction

Emptiness, the invisible, masculine,
makes Consciousness, the feminine,
pregnant, and the World is born
out of her.
Consciousness is so curious of the world,
and like Ouroboros, she has to explore.
She meets the World
in its masculine form,
and She has to devour,
be penetrated by the world.
Then She sees, She experiences
that She is it.

Da Capo Non Fine

168

You and I?

You are absolutely perfect for me,
because I love what you are in me.
Therefore, what I love is what I am –
and what I love is you,
remember?

On the other side of this,
if you open your eyes,
you will see how
all that you are,
is what you see.

To understand how this reveals
how we are one,
is wondrous indeed!
But to also allow
actually being All of it –
and
None of it…

… as there is nothing
to hold on to in The Void
… nothing
to hear in The Great Silence…
… not even
the Sound of Silence…

The above text began with
an anxiety about feeling unloved.
Can you see,
by experiencing
what the words above point to,
that there is no you and me,
in what is appearing in every Now –
and that anxiety about feeling unloved,
does not express my nature?

My nature is your nature.
Even though you may not see this,
let us at least, from now to always,
be absolutely certain, that:
You are absolutely perfect for me.
Da Capo Non Fine

Tetralemma

I am either
and both
and neither.

I am all contrast,
and all division,
and either,
and both,
and neither.

Sex, gender,
age, nationality, culture, age,
and all other labels,
contrasts and divisions
now falls in a different light.

I am light.

Beauty

Beauty
is the openness
to let the observer
see himself in you.

There is Love.

You are mine

That which Is
says:

Every expression of love
is how I tell you
how infinitely loved
you are.

Every longing in you
is My longing
that whispers
that you live in Me.

Every loss in you
is My loss
that shouts
that you are Mine.

The shadow

It is difficult to love
when I have forgotten
that Love is me

Love itself
flows freely
as I remember this

It flows
to the same extent
that I see this

But a scent
are all my attempts
to reflect this Love

But a shadow
is all I am
in this Love

Close

So holy
is Your every look,
whether fleeting or bottomless,
Your every touch,
whether light or enfolding.
Every word from Your lips,
is healing balm.

I receive
and can never repay.
All my doing
becomes a ceremony
in reverence of You
and Your gifts,
an honoring of my Beloved.

So close to You,
I see only myself
in Your eyes.
And in mine,
only You are seen.
You are me,
and I am You.

Possible

What makes it possible
to love myself,
is that what I am
contains what I love,
when I love myself.

Nature says

Animals have nests, no home.
The offspring of animals, by and large
manage on their own after birth.
Man, on the other hand, builds homes,
where families form,
where parents love unconditionally
and care for their children for very long.

Maybe this is a reflection
of something higher;
The Void that fecundates Consciousness:

From (masculine) emptiness
the (feminine) I Am appears.
By, in, and from I Am
a world is born.
I give birth to a world
every moment.
A world that I am,
and is in Me,
lives in Me, its home.
It is the born,
our beloved creation!
We love unconditionally
our family, our creation,
our world,
in which we see ourSelves.

The same

In this spaceless and timeless Love,
we are not the same —
we are one and the same.

Reminder

I cannot really ever love you.
The most I can do
is to remind you
that you are loved.
Eventually
you might remember
that you already are
the Love that you seek.
Then we don't need anything.
Then we are nothing,
which through the cycles of timelessness
in the worlds of Consciousness,
looks like this. Now.

Mysterious

What is mysterious
is not what I am,
but that I can believe
that I am something separate
from what I experience.

Then I can conjure up
a million ways
to try to find home
for what I am.
Which I already am.

To create such a mystery
is not my inclination
when I see that all this
is only myself.
As myself.

Love says

When I embrace you,
is it not Love that tells you
that you are security?

When I kiss you,
is it not Love that tells you
that you are closeness?

When you feel, with all your senses, that I love you,
is it not Love that tells you
that you are love?

Welcome

The fact that almost everyone
can fall in love with almost anyone
is a reflection of mySelf,
that loves everything – by, from, and as mySelf.

Everything in this feedback loop in mySelf,
which every experience confirms,
is in reality only mySelf,
loving mySelf.

In Me, everything is welcome,
and I mean everything!
Calling anything difficult
does not destroy or diminish Me.

To call anything euphoria
does not change or elevate Me.
I am only the space
where everything is welcome.

Be the same

The gaze of desire is not in my eyes.
Nor in yours.
Rather in both.

The caress is not in my hand.
Nor in your cheek.
Rather in both.

The kiss is not in my lips.
Nor in yours.
Rather in both.

What we experience, in all that we do,
is the meeting of seemingly two,
in the reality of being the same.

Yearning

My yearning for Love
is Love's yearning for me.
The yearning only stops
when we are one,
as I am It,
and It is I,
no longer two.

As such, I feel
everyone's yearning for Love,
absolutely every single one,
as I am also that, ever yearning…
I can hold it all,
as this Love
that holds all things.

Infatuation

I recognize this.
It is the very enjoyable experience
of infatuation.
But in reality,
infatuation is but one of many reminders
of the truth that we are already,
and have always been, one.
One in Love
that embraces and contains everything.
Infatuation, too.
Love loves to remind us
that we are Love,
that loves itself.
Like this.

Dream woman

A desire to give in, crack, burst
before her elusive beauty
and lustful play
that always ceases
when we are so close…

She haunts me in my dreams
but never intended to be found.
She knew already before we met
and told me in our play
what I had already begun to suspect…

I am her already.
I had thought I could find in another
what I already am.
The play becomes euphoria of Truth
and I give in, crack, burst…

The sum

I am what you need me to be.
Not because I make an effort,
no, fully automatically. Now. Because it is so.
I am less and less "the sum of my experiences,"
and more and more "the sum of your experiences of me,"
and everyone else's.
But yours are so close to me,
that I no longer see
or experience
any difference.

Heaven

Whether there are many bodies, or just this one present,
does not really change anything. I am still what I am.

If I start to think that "I am this lonesome body of mine,"
then shortly thereafter, the feeling of loneliness will arise.

But I remember my Beloved, that I am always and still
exactly what I am. I am that I am.

As that I am, all I know is experiencing
what can be called this World.

This experience is so intimate, I cannot separate myself from it,
and I realize that I am this.

Any identification that involves forgetting this, is perfectly okay for a while,
but I am constantly reminded that I am always and still exactly that I am.

Forgetting this has been called Hell.
Remembering this is, and has always been called Heaven.

Remember, every child in this World, whence you came!
And we sit together in Heaven.

Free mind

A free mind can take me anywhere.
I can go with it, to amazing places,
and go anywhere, but always nowhere,
because I am always right here,
regardless of every experience.

If there is another mind that walks with mine
or not – really makes no difference.
I am not in mind, mind is in me,
so naturally, I can do without mind,
but mind cannot do without me.

Did I think that mind matters,
and that finding a kindred mind is important?
My mind changes all the time,
why wouldn't everyone else's?
I am the constant, in which everything changes.

Mind can feel lonely, in weaving yet more stories.
But only until it is informed by what I am,
that what I am, is what every "I" is.
Alone, all one, yes, and in my Self
is every other and no other.

Beauty

It is not what I think is beautiful that is beautiful to experience,
it is beautiful to experience beauty.
It is also beautiful to be what is beautiful,
the experience of being the other side of myself.
And I know this as this other side.
Because beauty is everything.

To film the experience

Background

Lucid dreaming is now a common occurrence for me: In the dream, knowing that I am dreaming, and then be able to "decide" what happens in the dream, who I want to talk to, or what I want to do in the dream – just as I do when awake.

In the beginning of 2019, I sit a few weeks and meditate on lucid dreaming. I ponder: If I can go from deep dreamless sleep to lucid dreaming, can I also go from being awake to lucid dreaming? It should not be different, other than instead of moving around with dreamed characters and things, I would move around in the world with physical characters and things. In this state of lucidly dreaming, would I be able "decide" what will happen, what I want to do, etc?

I set out to do an experiment – to go from being awake to lucidly dreaming, in this case about something very specific, something that has fascinated and almost spellbound me since a very early age, something that I never really understood… What does this fascination really consist of? In lucidly dreaming, maybe I can explore this fascination, what it really is, just like I do about other things when lucidly dreaming in sleep.

I record this my first experience, position the camera phone so it can record what happens. This in order to possibly determine if what happened really looks like it was authentically experienced, and to "document" it, similar to what I do with my writing.

I prepare a "scene" with things that I feel are necessary to lucidly dream about this fascination. Then I sit with the "props" and am open to the possibility that I begin to lucidly dream about it.

It is not difficult, and completely without effort, the boundary between awake and lucidly dreaming disappears. Then it all happens – I almost throw myself over the props, and I am no longer only observing, but I perform myself what I had been so fascinated by! The boundary between me and the props disappears, I am sucked in like into a whirlwind where the props and my activities whirl around. In this experience, I am not only the one watching, I am both the "actor" and the props simultaneously, that's what it feels like, and there are no thoughts about which is which. There is nothing outside and nothing inside the experience, I am it and simultaneously both the actor and the props – **and** the one watching! I am very familiar with only watching since my youth, but now… Wow! So it becomes clear now, in this "awake" lucid dreaming, that what I am so fascinated with, is not only watching it, but to feel what it is like to be both the actor and the props.

When the activities cease and the experience of being both the actor and the observer recedes, I turn off the phone and fall, exhausted and shocked, onto the couch and just stare for several hours.

When I later play back what was recorded, on a larger screen, I get the next shock. Not only does it definitely look like it was authentically experienced, it is also very easy to be completely absorbed by it and feel what I felt when recording it: To simultaneously be both the actor, the props, and the observer!

I repeat this experiment a few days later. Same thing. Repeat again, same thing. Before the following occasions, I alter the "scene," removing distracting things and adding things that fit the scene even better. Every experiment turns out to be even more absorbing, both while recording and when I watch it on the big screen afterward.

I make about twenty of these videos in a year, videos that no one else sees, and that I can talk to no one about – I barely know myself what I am doing! I have not seen anything like this before, but to some degree, I recognize something that I have heard others talk about regarding specifically film art, directors and others. So I fumble about on the internet, to maybe find others who would understand what I am doing – maybe to be mirrored in their experience, and maybe to get some pointers to how I can film it even better – so I upload a few videos to a small group of creators of film art, and they watch them, but I don't tell them anything about how the videos came to be.

Then I get my third shock… They absolutely love the videos, and they report that they, too, become enraptured, engrossed, and that something very unusual happens to them – they feel what I feel in front of the camera! How is this possible?

In many conversations with a couple of these people, who are also well versed in philosophy and non-dualism, I hear how they see it. I had not been thinking about it in this way before, I had been so busy making more videos, but sure, I can understand what they say.

Here are a couple of examples that seem to agree with the experience:

1. Art is ultimately such that it is said to be able to "transport" the observer into what the artist experienced when he created the artwork, that the boundary between the artist and the observer disappears, and that the observer "becomes" the artist when observing.

2. The experience of the absence of this boundary between what experiences and what is experienced, is what the "old texts," the perennial philosophy, e.g. parts of the Bhagavad Gita, define as the Tantric path to "awakening."

All this is very agreeable to me, but I really don't care so much about what I hear from them, while for sure, there is now some intellectual confirmation of my experiment. While filming, on the other hand, the intellect is not particularly active at all.

So after this, I don't really do anything else than make videos. I get more props and equipment and refine my methods of filming. By now, there are about 60–70 videos, all between a half hour to two hours long, which each took two to seven days to produce.

The small group of creators of film art has grown, and they still look forward to more videos. Some of them make their own videos, and we exchange valuable viewpoints. A handful of them say that they feel roughly the same about the experience, and about how intense it is.

I bend over backwards many times to make the videos in such a way that what is filmed can be even closer to the experience. A couple of times, I am on my way to see others who could be my cameramen and take care of the practical things, which is very complicated and strenuous to do alone – it takes so much energy and attention – but for various reasons, this does not happen.

The experience is always there, even when I am not filming. The "mystique" and intensity in the experience is undeniable. And apparently, it is possible to experience the same thing when watching the video, regardless if one has lived in India or Brazil one's whole life.

But here's yet another aspect of all this:
The experience – to experience oneself as both what experiences, what is experienced, and the observer simultaneously – is not reserved for me, artists, or mystics! One could think that it would require years of training, certain props, certain methods, etc, to attain something unusual. But of course not, and that is not how it was for me, either. The experience is always available, regardless if I am sitting very close to my friend while looking into each others' eyes, if I stand alone watching the sunrise after having woken up in a tent that I raised in the dark night before, if I after a long day at work end up in the couch with my favorite music in the speakers… To "become one with every-thing" may sound like the most exotic and esoteric experience, but it is also the most familiar of experiences. It does not happen "out there," it happens in here, in what I really am, hitherto, "on this side of" experience. Every time.

Only mind, as usual, can "get in the way". A thought may come, and I can believe it, that things need to be in a particular way in order to generate this experience – but I dare suggest that if mind is open to the possibility that what I really **am** – this side of experience, without labels, valuation, thoughts, or conditioning – is what is always experiencing everything that is experienced, in my Self, of my Self, by and as my Self… and then, it doesn't matter **what** I experience, because I already am both that which experiences and what is experienced, **and** the observer! Always both. Simultaneously.

What am I filming?

I film the experience. The expressions I film are of a certain kind, because they happen by and through my mind, and my mind is also of a certain kind, due to conditioning, learned behaviors, likes and tastes, preferences, etc. This holds true of all minds, of course, so my mind is no different than anyone else's in this regard. When others create similar "works of art," they happen under different circumstances, and the content of the experience and the videos are different – but the experience of the dissolution of the boundary between what visually might look like two, subject and object, is the same.

In my mind, there is no longer the experience of only one gender, but of both the masculine and feminine, and they are so intimately intertwined that the experience of both, is actually **one** experience. I have concluded that this means a couple of things:

My mind is neither masculine nor feminine, and not masculine plus feminine, either. My mind is neither, but it can give space for and express what it is like to **be** both the masculine and feminine, simultaneously. This does not make me masculine or feminine, neither both, yet I experience what it is like to be both, simultaneously. Both happen in, and is experienced by what I am. This difference may sound semantic, but is actually the foundation of the realization of what I am, and of what there is a possibility or capacity to contain and give expression for. On this foundation, I feel no need to identify as either gender, nor as any other. Identification simply has no meaning to me any longer.

In a way, this can be likened to what it is like to be an actor who can play and "be" any character on stage or on film, but does not identify as any of them.

Because both the masculine and the feminine is expressed and experienced through my mind, there is no "need" for another mind in what I do. The masculine and feminine have already "married" each other, become one in what I feel, experience, and do, and therefore, it is both an expression for and a celebration of the consummation of this true matrimony. It is through innumerable experiences that I discover this, so it is not non-sense or naive fantasies. I can really only do one thing in my film art, and that is to be true to this experience.

A little later, this strikes me:

If what I do is art, my art is symbolism.
This art contains symbols
for a select few human experiences,
and not for any others.

It follows, then,
that my intention has never been
for anyone to fall in love with my art,
but with what my art points to.

Art is the communication of ecstasy.

P.D. Ouspensky (1878–1947)

Below are texts that were written soon after experiencing this.

I am you

I want to be you
embracing me.
Now I am you,
embracing me.

Since forever
I wanted to be
what attracted me most.
Now I am that!

Kiss

When our mouths kiss,
are your lips kissing mine,
or are my lips kissing yours?
Both!

Culmination

–The culmination
of me loving you,
and of you loving me,
is when we no longer
know the difference.
–What difference?
–Exactly!

Love

I don't see what I love,
I love what I see.
I don't feel what I love,
I love what I feel.

Picture

More than a thousand words
sometimes say nothing
about a picture.

In me

I feel you
I feel you inside me
I feel you pulsating inside me
Show me what it is like
to be inside me!

The circle

The masculine in me receives
all your feminine graces,
everything you give so lustfully.
I receive exactly that which I would give,
had I your attributes.

As you offer up your luscious gifts,
I am compelled to be inside you,
and your lust for that draws me in,
so that I can experience what it is like
to give all that you give me.

So I come into you,
all I want is to be inside you,
so I can feel what it is like
to open up, to give my whole being,
so I can feel what it is like to be you.

When inside you, and you inside me,
this turns out to be
one and the same experience,
and all there is,
is One experiencing all.

The experience of myself

I am not both.
"Both" is what I look like,
only an appearance.
I am all and everything,
anyway.

Seeing both,
is separating that which
cannot be separated,
because it is everything,
and everything consists of it.

It is experiencing itself
as the appearance of both.

As I devour myself,
I am not actually devouring myself,
I am what looks like both,
both the devourer and the devoured,
but always – it is only I.

To experience this unity,
this oneness of myself,
is the dissolution of the idea
that there could be two.

As I devour
what seems to be myself,
I am realizing,
beyond a shadow of a doubt,
that all there is,
is I.

This non-union of what is not two
is therefore what is most satisfying
for my seemingly separate appearing entity,
which, in reality, only is I.
To realize, feel, and experience this,
is the experience of myself.

Trance

I fell into trance when I watched a certain kind of film,
so I wanted to experience what was experienced in it:
The dissolution of separation,
when what looked like two,
merged and proved to be one.

I needed to be what becomes one,
to be both, and merge into one.
I crossed the illusory, thin boundary between the two,
and dissolved with it, in the boundlessness that followed.
When I am both, I am one.

I recorded my own film, precisely that kind of film.
I filmed the experience of
the dissolution of separation.
When I watch the film afterward,
I feel and see that everything is always one. Like I am.

I am she!

I have discovered that I am also the feminine
that loves to experience what I love.

Then she is my experience.
When she is my experience, she is I.

I am the love whereby she loves me.
She is the love whereby I love her.

Completely without separation.
She is I, and I am she.

There is no boundary or separation
between what I love and what she does,
between what she loves and what I do.

We are one and the same,
in what is experienced,
this side of all boundaries.

Art

What the visual artist is doing
is trying to communicate how he sees what is seen.
Seeing is not difficult, he simply sees.
But to communicate it,
he must eliminate in his art what he doesn't see.
And that is difficult.

On the other side…

When the observer experiences
how the artist saw what was seen,
it is not a communication of anything,
but it is one seeing, being one and the same.
In this one and the same seeing,
there is no separation.

Beauty

Beauty simply is. We are taught to think that it is the objects that are beautiful, but are they really?

What is called Beautiful by one, may be called Ugly by another, so the beauty cannot be a property of the object.

But this does not "prove" that Beauty is subjective, because Beauty needs no proof, nor can it be proven. Beauty is simply present when beheld, when experienced – and because it is experienced, it is undeniably true – completely regardless of the object, which is rather only a door into Beauty itself. The door is in this way uninteresting for the one who has walked through it, into Beauty itself.

Beauty is not inherent in the object seen, but experienced in the beholder.

Thus, it is said:
"Beauty is in the beholder"

and

"If the doors of perception were cleansed,
every thing would appear to man as it is, Infinite."

Talent

A friend said about my videos:
–"I think there's no other person in the world with your talent."

I answered:
Hang-on, there's no competition, and talents cannot be compared. Everyone is the best. At being what they are. No one else can be me, and no one else can be you! Or could, **ever**! I just happen to know **and** feel **and** dare to be and do what I love. And everyone can do that!

No idea

As free even from freedom itself,
I have no idea
what will happen.

If I would know what is going to happen,
it would be my conditioned and usual assessments
and preconceived ideas.

Preconceived ideas about how one should live
then become what determines what will happen.
And what happens becomes rather predictable.

But free also from freedom itself,
I have no idea
what will happen.

About time?

It's about time that I – after having felt what it is like to be the masculine for so many years – now can feel what it is like to be the feminine!

And this is not a contradiction, rather the opposite – just as a coin would not be a coin without both its sides. Now I know and feel that I am the coin.

One experience

When I caress my thigh with my hand,
I simultaneously feel
both what it is like to caress a thigh
and what it is like to have my thigh caressed.
It is not strange to feel both,
because both these experiences
are in fact one experience.
The separating it into two experiences
only happens afterward in the mind.

When I hold your hand,
there is no separation in this experience either.
That we both can say that we experience it,
tells us that we are the same that experiences,
not that we are separate.
The experience is indivisible,
and so is that which experiences.
This is not strange.
Separation is strange.

Close

Not until I feel so close to you
that I no longer see anyone else but myself,
and not until you feel so close to me
that you no longer see anyone else but yourself,
do we feel at home,
where no one needs to be
anyone else but oneself.
The same self.

I am this

There are two ways to say "I am this"
These two ways are direct opposites of each other.
We could say it with this emphasis:
"I am **this**".
That is to say that it is **this** that is me.
This is how I learned to say it, and thus how I thought,
and I was not aware that it could be said
in two different and opposing ways.

So what is the other way to say "I am this"?
Well, with this emphasis:
"**I am** this".
That is to say, it is **I who am** this.

The second way to say it
is actually the only true way.
It describes something true,
because it matches our experience.
I am this. It is I who am… this.

In this way, **this** is not I,
because it is **I who am**… this.
Everything contained in the concept "this"
is something that I am, it is I who am it,
but not the other way around – it is not I.

The same goes for you.
You are… this.
Not the other way around.
And because I am… this,
and you are… this,
you and I are the same,
that which is this.
I am the same I that you are.
You are the same I that I am.

That which experiences this
is not this,
but that which experiences this.

If I say "I am **this**" the first way,
it is the first and greatest mistake in history,
that is to say that I would be **this**,
for example my body,
and that you would be some other **this**,
for example your body.
The obvious consequence is then
that I have to defend what I believe I am,
if there were a fight between you and me.
I may even come to think that it is necessary
to create weapons to defend myself from you…

If, on the other hand, I say "**I am** this" the other way,
that is to say that all this is something that I am,
for example your and my body,
the obvious consequence is then
that I am careful with this,
because it is I who is… this.
Because if I do something bad to this,
I am doing something bad to myself,
since it is I who is… this.

There is a lot to these words:
"Love thy neighbor as yourself"
because I am… my neighbor.

My Lover

I have met my Lover.
My Lover is the Love
whereby I love my Lover.

My Lover loves me so intimately
that I no longer feel any difference
between my Lover and myself.

My Lover is my all.
There is nothing
but my Lover.

My Lover and I are one,
as I am one with everything that I love,
knowing full well that my Lover is the Love
whereby I love everything.

Love myself

When I have come to love myself
more than anyone else
could ever love me,
what do I do then?
And how, then, could I
ever need to have
a relationship with anyone?

Reversed again

I don't like something because it looks good,
it's the other way around – again.
We could stop here, but let us investigate.

If I look at something that I have experienced before,
something that feels very good to do or participate in,
then I like to look at it.
The experience is always prior to the opinion that it looks good.
So – it looks good because I like it.

Like?

We don't like what we like,
we like the liking.

I want you inside me!

When the feminine feels "I want you inside me!,"
she is an order of magnitude down from Consciousness,
which says to the seemingly separate person
"I want you in Me!"

This does not mean that the seemingly separate person
isn't already in Consciousness,
but Consciousness says this as a concession
to the person who sees and feels himself as separate.

This is how the poets and mystics wrote
"Lord, you are the Love whereby I love you".
So in all of this experience, there is nothing but Love.

But this Love is not all sugary sweet!
This Love is what allows for separation,
to believe that we are separate,
and that we therefore even have to make war
against what we think is "another".

But remember what a carpenter said long ago:
"Love thy neighbor as thyself"
which means to love my neighbor
because he **is** myself.

So, when the feminine says "I want you inside me!"
it is a reflection from above, from god himself if you wish.

So what is the masculine who penetrates a reflection of?
It represents the seemingly separate person,
that only really wants to be inside what he consists of.
He consists of the feminine that says
"I want you inside me!"

When this is all said and done, consummated,
something miraculous happens:
The feminine divides her own body into a baby!
The baby's sole purpose in life
is going to be, and is, and will always be,
to find his or her way back,
back to what he consists of.

As we know, most of us replace
being the Love that we love with,
or we confuse it with
substances, relationships, sensations,
and we believe that whatever it is that we yearn for,
it is outside ourselves and we have to reach for it,
work hard to get it,
and in a sense waste our whole lives
in this search for something external.

But here's "mother" again,
mother to all us "siblings"
who are all brought up to feel as though
we are separate persons,
and all we have ever done that really matters,
is finding our way back to "her".

To feel this feminine in sexuality,
is something that the "male" mind
could never fathom –
to be on the receiving end
of someone coming inside
what he really is.

And the circle of life
incessantly goes around and around…

Remembering

Now I remember what You told me before I was made!
I thank You for enduing me with this role of mine.

In the light of what You told me before I was made,
my role has developed into this, where there is nothing left
in me, or of me, or out of me, me and my feeble mind.
With nothing left in me, You can shine, oh Highest,
You are my fulfillment, a fulfillment that tells me
that I never left Your side.

All there is when I am in You – and that is always –
is Your shining through everything that happens,
either for me to learn or for me to experience,
this perfect experience where I am no longer man or woman,
but only Spirit, as both the masculine and feminine,
simultaneously.

Fully known

I am he, expressing every sexual desire for her.
I am she, yearning for his every expression of sexuality.

I am he, compelled to be inside her, to know her intimately.
I am she, yearning to be filled up by him, to be intimately known.

When he is inside her, he feels what it is like
to be her, yearning to be filled up, to be fully known.

When she has him inside her, she feels what it is like
to be him, knowing her fully.

When fully known,
we are no longer two.

…then shall I know even as also I am known
1 Corinthians 13:12

*There is neither Jew nor Greek, there is neither bond nor free, there is neither **male** nor **female***
Galatians 3:28

One friend who understands what I am doing in my film art, expresses something about the beauty he experiences, and says that it is in my eyes. To this, I reply:

Meeting

If my physical eye-balls were laying next to someone else's, they would not look much different from each other. So it is not the eye-balls that we meet.

It is I – what I really am – who look through my eyes, and when you – what you really are – see this through your eyes, that which is seeing, meets… itself. That which sees me, is what is seeing you – the only I there is – seeing itself. It seems that this is possible also through this medium, film. We could call it mystical, but it is real in a truer sense than the physical. Only in this meeting, lies the beauty, and nowhere else.

The fact that the same meeting is not experienced when someone else is watching the same video doe not change this truth.

The fact that it is my eyes in particular that you are looking into, does not change anything either. The meeting and the beauty in the meeting is always there, when that which sees… sees itSelf.

After almost four years of film art, there has been a lot of correspondence with my "audience". I can surmise that it is extremely few that has seen my art for what it is, or rather what it points to. Maybe this is the case for most artists. Below are a couple of texts that were written in response:

Humiliation?

About "guilt" and "humiliation" and how they are related.

I understand that both are learned. Humiliation is a way to avoid feeling guilt. So when I no longer feel guilt, there is no need for humiliation. Sexuality is so sacred all by itself, and as such, it needs no explanation or justification, no mental assessment or judgment, and it draws one into a freedom of expression that is prior to mind.

Objectification

Regarding objectifying and worshipping me and/or my art, this quote from the film *Ready Player One* (2018) is very clear:

Parzival: I said I'm in love with you.
Art3mis: No, you're not. You only know what I want you to know. You only see what I want you to see. That's what you're in love with.

In my films, I am merely a muse. Neither my expressions, nor myself, are what they point to. I do not encourage worship of the muse, nor its expressions – I encourage worship of Love itself.

Love scene

This is taking place in the movie *Sucker Punch* from 2011, and it captures something deep:

High Roller: –You see, I am what you might call a man who has everything. And yet, I lack the one thing money can't buy.

Baby Doll: –Love?

High Roller: –Close. Truth is more accurate. I seek a true moment, a moment of truth. In this world of lies. It just so happens that… that moment, that fragile, delicate thing, like a glass egg or a sand castle, well, that moment can only be given by a non-faker. A non-actor. That's you.

Baby Doll: –I don't understand.

High Roller: −Well, I have spent a small fortune getting you in this room. This golden cage. You're supposed to give yourself to me. It's completely physical. I might have your body but the real you, that intangible, and indefinable spark that is you… Well, that you I will never know. And, yet, that is precisely what I want.

Baby Doll: −I'm sorry. You seem really nice. You want me to lie to you?

High Roller: −No, I don't. All I require from you is a sliver of a moment. To have you not by force but simply as a man and a woman. To see in your eyes that simple truth that you give yourself to me freely. Not because you have to, but because you want to. Now, of course, for such a gem, I will give as well. I'm willing to give you freedom. Pure and total freedom. Freedom from the drudgery of every day life, freedom… that abstract ideal. Freedom from pain, freedom from responsibility, freedom from guilt, from regret, freedom from sadness, freedom from loss, the freedom to be happy − don't close your eyes, I need you to look at me − the freedom to love.

I have learned so much from God

I
Have
Learned
So much from God
That I can no longer
Call
Myself A Christian, a Hindu, a Muslim
A Buddhist, a Jew.

The Truth has shared so much of Itself
With me
That I can no longer call myself
A man, a woman, an angel
Or even pure
Soul.

Love has
Befriended Hafez so completely
It has turned to ash
And freed
Me
Of every concept and image
My mind has ever known.

Hafez (1325−1389)

CHAPTER 8

Last words?

I asked myself this:
– Did I think that it would have consequences to realize what I truly Am, now that I understand how radically differently my mind was conditioned? Of course!

– Do I then also understand that the more different, and the longer and deeper the conditioning, the more radical the realization and its consequences? Yes!

In my personal life, I see this realization as a revolution, but at the same moment, I feel so right at home, like I never left, and that I was never separate from anything, least of all from reality. And I see that only after this revolution, I can now rest completely and always in seeing this, even when my mind at times still reaches for something in the illusory land of concepts that we call the past and future.

Only now can I be free to be whatever I Am and to do what I do, without worrying about or trying to achieve something I was supposed to be or do, neither according to my own nor the preconceived ideas of others.

Completely naturally, consequences happen, as seen from my mind's old patterns, but seeing it from what I know I Am, all events flow through Being, like everything else. Action has turned from reactive through the filters of the mind, to only active seeing.

All is said and done, Fait Accompli, complete. Now, anything can happen – like it always could, and did! I am no longer damaged or diminished by anything that happens, as I see that it happens in me, and not against me. And this is so clear, even if doubts would appear in the mind. This seeing is more real than believing that it is not.

Finally – as seen from mind's perspective – love, compassion, empathy, inclusion, and acceptance can flow naturally from and in this seeing, as opposed to the seeing through filters. And none of it needs my nor anyone else's attention, confirmation, or recognition. What a relief!

All activities that previously were designed by mind to gain whatever was thought to be missing or lacking, are now freed from any such efforts, free to just happen, in harmony with and informed by the understanding of what I truly Am. Not that mind should be blamed for anything, it only acted out of its own conditioned ideas that were planted generations ago in an unfathomably complex web of relations, a web that is impossible to chart.

Seeing that there never was a personal ground to neither stand on nor to hold on to, but rather that this is one and the same ground for all beings – I cannot but humbly bow to how the Being is the same, the ground from which all that is manifest is born. This leaves no room for any personal agenda nor identity developed by the mind, because all that is simply not needed any longer, as mind never had that task. Instead, mind can now serve its only purpose; to be my beloved servant, in service of my body and the world – in what I Am.

Aging...

One could think that the older my body gets, the faster I move toward death. Every year is equally long on the calendar, but it can seem that the years go faster, or that the steps toward death become successively shorter after, say, age fifty. But actually, fifty is around half of "life," and when half is left, that isn't old, is it? The perception of how long a year is seems to decrease almost logarithmically.

(If we search for an explanation to this, it is surely found in that one year is half of a two-year-old's life, but only a fiftieth of a fifty-year-old, so it is pretty obvious that the fifty-year-old would perceive a year as shorter than when he was two years old)

What happens then, around fifty, is often that we work hard to prolong life, to become 120 or 130 years old, if successful. We work to prolong life with maybe pills, surgery, gene therapy, etc. If we make sure that we live to be 130, we may think that it feels like "half left" then. Think!

All this energy, research, etc, that is spent on prolonging life (from little things like "anti-aging cream" all the way to gene therapy), is based on how aging and death is viewed by the middle-aged − but we really have no idea about what it will be or feel like when we are around 100.

My strong hunch is that if I were to ask someone who is now 120 after having successfully prolonged his life, "Would you rather **not** have had these extra years?," he would probably answer "Yes, why ever did I get these extra years...?"

The perceived length of my life has nothing to do with how other people die or how old they are when they do − it is not a process of comparison that makes me feel that I would want to prolong life.

But above all, the question about "prolonging life" misses something larger: Life has no opposite. Its opposite is not death. The opposite of death is birth. Life contains them both, and the activity, process, the illusory person Mischa, happens in between. That life can end is not even hearsay, but only a learned and preconceived idea. What we call life, is the closest relative to Consciousness; that all we know and see, is that we are. And because we really are, I am reminded of:

That which is, never ceases to be;
that which is not, never comes into existence.

Bhagavad Gita

What is aging, then?

Accumulating experiences. Nothing else.

Questions?

I haven't really gotten answers to any questions.
I just don't have any questions anymore.

Care?

I don't care about what I do.
I do what I care about.

Truth

If you see
that what I say
is True,
then you also know
that it is not My form
that says it,
but Truth itself.

Salutation

I salute all my young friends!
Only after having associated with you
who don't care about age,
have I finally understood
that age doesn't matter.

Forgive?

The world turns
on the friendly smile I give you
as we pass each other in the crowd,
as I thank each and every one of you
for what you have made me,
and I forgive you
for everything you did or didn't do.

All I am is the love
that encompasses everything and everyone
that has ever been part of my earthly life.
I could not do anything else than what I did,
and neither could you.
It is all just the tapestry of what we call our lives.

Had I been you, I would have done the same.
Had you been me, you would have done the same.
So in reality, there is no forgiveness, nor guilt.
All that has ever been, is what is.
Which I am. And you.

Matthew 6:12
And forgive us our debts, as we forgive our debtors.

When I die

When I die, when my coffin is being taken out
You must never think I am missing this world.
Don't shed any tears, don't lament or feel sorry.
I'm not falling into a monster's abyss.

When you see my corpse is being carried,
Don't cry for my leaving.
I'm not leaving, I'm arriving at eternal love.

When you leave me in the grave, don't say goodbye.
Remember a grave is only a curtain for the paradise behind.
You'll only see me descending into a grave, now watch me rise!

How can there be an end? When the sun sets
Or the moon goes down, it looks like the end,
It seems like a sunset, but in reality it is a dawn.

When the grave locks you up, that is when your soul is freed.
Have you ever seen a seed fallen to earth not rise with a new life?
Why should you doubt the rise of a seed named human?…
When for the last time you close your mouth,
Your words and soul will belong to the world of no place, no time.

Rumi (1207-1273)

When Mischa is dead

You may find me whenever and wherever. Maybe you find my dead body – poor you. But you should know that what you see then, is not me. I am and I have always been what experiences everything, yes, my body that once babbled, and also what you are experiencing right now. Know therefore, that I am with and in you always, yes, I even **am** the same you that you are. Even if you are looking at a dead body, with noticeable wrinkles and completely empty eyes, maybe the snus has run down, the beard grown – don't be ashamed by what you see, don't be afraid, sad, or worried. I Am, and will always be. The same as you are. Beloved, in unspeakable and boundless love, we are contained in each other!

And never forget this,
ponder it when you leave this place,
tomorrow and every day:
That which saw you when we were talking,
is what sees my coffin now.
And that which saw me then,
is what saw you then.
And now.

The search is over

I can die in peace now

Every moment
that I don't do that
I celebrate in unspeakable gratitude
and reverence for
what Is
with the Song of Being

Illustrations

Background of cover: *From within the Sälskär lighthouse, Åland 2012*, by the author.

Front cover: *Drawing Hands*, 1948,
lithograph by the Dutch artist M. C. Escher (1898–1972).

Back cover: Selfie by the author, 2021.

Page 1: *Birth*, 2022, by Hild Krusell.

Page 15: *Universal indicator solutions in a lab*, by Stephen Gibson,
from sciencestockphotos.com, creative commons.

Page 45: *Lightship free photo by Bert Hardy*, 1941, from freeimages.com.

Page 129: *Silhouette of Man Standing Beside Ocean during Sunset*,
Ali Naderi, from pexels.com, creative commons.

Page 139: *Brick*, outside Lasse Åberg's "Mus-eum," 2004, Bålsta, by the author.

Page 162: *The Treachery of Images*, 1929,
oil painting by the Belgian artist René Magritte (1898–1967).

Page 165: *Imagination?*, by the author, 2022.

Page 195: *Close-Up Photo Of Book Pages*, Ravi Kant, from pexels.com, creative commons.

Thank you…

…to all friends who in so many and different ways have been on my path. You have
been so close to my heart through so many fantastic and valuable events that I don't feel
anything but gratitude for being. No one mentioned, no one forgotten…

Special thanks to…

Hild Krusell for insights and input.

Karl-Erik Nilsson for insights, input, and proofreading the Swedish version of this book.

Easter egg

To the reader: I encourage you to take notes, pose questions, and comment in the book.
There is quite a bit of white space for that. I you send your book with notes to me, I can
learn and see in new ways by reading them – and I promise to send you a new book! I'm
sure you can get in touch with me by using a suitable search engine on the web!

Glossary

During my theological studies, I became fascinated by language and how it is used, and I tried to find out what the intent was, what was intended to express when a certain word or expression was first formed and began to be used.

In the development of language, it turns out that certain words have even developed an opposite or quite different meaning, they have come to express something foreign to the times when the word was first used.

One such example is the word school. It comes from the Greek *skholē* which means spare time, leisure, rest, ease. That is to say when one is free. Free from what? Well, when e.g. the children that worked with the adults in the fields had some time off, they were often eager to go to the places where the learned communicated wisdom and knowledge, often outside libraries, as they wanted to improve their understanding. The younger kids were aided by the older kids, later slaves, that escorted them to these places. One such "role" also got a name; *paidagōgos*, from the Greek *pais* = children + *agōgos* = lead. How *skholē* later came to be used for something quite opposed that is forced onto children, and how *paidagōgos* came to be used for someone who instructs teachers, is interesting…

I have found my discoveries about the origin of words beneficial in two ways.

1. I often find that what was intended to express from the beginning has been lost in the modern usage of language, and that a lost meaning can point to something valuable.
2. When what was intended to express has been lost in modern use of language, it becomes difficult to express what has been lost, because now, there are no other words for it. Even worse, maybe even the possibility to experience or feel what was originally expressed gets lost. Example: I have begun to suspect that the experience that the word equanimity points to – an experience of "evenness of mind, calmness; good-will, kindness" (see etymonline.com) – is becoming more rare, and that both the word and the experience that it points to, will get lost.

I heard somewhere that *As the language is, we think* and that it goes hand in hand with *As we think, the language becomes*. As I see it, there is therefore reason to investigate the origin of words and concepts.

In this glossary, I make no language science claims. My reference is most often *Online Etymology Dictionary*. It has its flaws, but does point in a direction that has helped me in my passion for words and the function and origin of language.

The first time a word in the glossary is used in the book, it is marked with an asterisk.

Attention

From the Latin *ad* + *tendere* = stretch toward. To direct one's perception and/or thought activity to a specific thing, e.g. an apple or a thought. In modern language use, the word consciousness is often used instead of attention – but consciousness is independent of attention, and attention is obviously dependent on consciousness, which is primary. Example: The sensory organ senses a sound (true). I/Awareness experience a sound (true). I/mind perceive a sound (true). I/mind then direct my attention toward the sound – or not (true). I/mind then form an opinion about the sound – or not (true). The opinion about the sound can be true or not.

Brahman

Wikipedia: "the highest universal principle, the ultimate reality in the universe."
In hinduism, the word points to what I call Consciousness or Awareness.

Concept

From the Latin *con* + *capere*, with + grasp, take, i.e. conclusion, often a concrete expression for something abstract, with the intent to understand or explain the abstract. A synonym is "thought construction". It is fundamental that a concept can never describe experience. Two examples: 1) "America" is a concept. To say "I am in America" is based on a collection of information from which a conclusion is made, a construction only in thought, not from experience. 2) Time is a concept that tries to describe how we experience change in the world of things. But "time" says nothing about the experience of change. From the perspective of mind, time can be described as something that has its own existence that can be experienced, but it is not so. Everyone's experience of change is to be, to remember, and to think about "the future," and all this takes place in the now, not "in time".

Consciousness

Online Etymology Dictionary: from assimilated Latin form of *com* "with," or "thoroughly" + *scire* "to know".

The presence of that which is conscious, i.e. what we consist of. Here is referred to consciousness that knows, that is to say completely regardless of capacity to respond to stimuli (see below). Consciousness is present also in deep sleep, general anesthesia, and coma, even when the knowing is not about objects or thoughts. Note that I always use Consciousness without the definite article "the". To say "the consciousness," may sound like there could be more than one. Consciousness is not personal, either.

I also make a distinction between consciousness and attention, where the latter is an activity that has a beginning and an end, whereas the former does not. Consciousness is what is primary, fundamental for attention and all activities of and in the mind.

Whatever we are conscious **of,** is not and cannot be Consciousness, which must be present before consciousness **of** something at all can take place. I use *Consciousness* and *Awareness* interchangeably.

Control

My intuition tells me that *control* did not originally mean *to run, direct, govern,* which is how it is often used today.

Online Etymology Dictionary: early 15c., countrollen, "to check the accuracy of, verify; to regulate," from Latin contra "against" (see contra) + rotulus, diminutive of rota "wheel" (see roll (n.)). The word apparently comes from a medieval method of checking accounts by a duplicate register. Sense of "dominate, direct, exercise control over" is from mid-15c.

The sense *to direct* is therefore relatively new.

Conclusion: Verify against: It is the balance of things that makes it possible for both plus and minus to exist.

The "counter roll" as a metaphor: Everything on the one "roll" (Consciousness) is transferred onto the other "roll" (the World), and the pattern on both rolls is identical. In this process, neither beginning nor end can be observed or interpreted. We cannot really speak of the one actually transferring to another roll, because they are identical, in total balance and harmony, in a dance that looks like the pattern, the pattern that is seen as the relative; mind, thoughts, perceptions, emotions, etc, and the material universe. Such was the original intention behind the word.

Da Capo Non Fine

In musical notation, *Da Capo Al Fine* – From beginning to end – is used. I use it playfully to express that the text does not have an end, that it continues again from the beginning, and that it can be read and understood that way.

Dualism

Wikipedia: "Property dualism, a view in the philosophy of mind and metaphysics which holds that, although the world is composed of just one kind of substance – the physical kind – there exist two distinct kinds of properties: physical properties and mental properties."

Existence

From the Latin *exsistere, ex* = out from + *stare* = to stand. The meaning begs the question "Standing out from what?" Everything "stands out from" Consciousness, which means that all things have or borrow their reality from Consciousness – in, from and by which they are made. Nothing can be outside of or consist of anything else than that which is primary: Consciousness.

Experience

Online Etymology Dictionary: from Latin *experientia* 'a trial, proof, experiment; knowledge gained by repeated trials'.

In philosophical contexts, it is often replaced by "qualia," used the first time in English in 1929. Qualia is described as "instances of subjective, conscious experience," which often is indescribable, e.g. the flavor of an apple.

In this book I prefer to use the concept "direct experience" to emphasize that it is the nameless, label-less, and intellectually indescribable experience. The direct experience is always true, but when it is intellectually interpreted and described, the description can never truly represent the **direct** experience. The interpretation and describing of an experience always happens afterward, and is colored by culture, conditioning, memories, etc. The description is then more of an opinion than an experience.

In modern language use, the word is often confused with "perception" – but experience always happens before the interpretation of it is formed and expressed. (The forming and expression of a perception is also an experience, though!) I suspect that the modern use of the word has come from an intuition that an experience is unquestionable, unlike a perception. Example: "It is my **experience** that you threaten me" is really about a perception that happens in me under certain circumstances, so it would be more correct to say "It is my **perception** that you threaten me" (or even more clear and true: "I feel threatened"). "I experience a bird singing" would be expressed more correctly "I perceive that the sound I that hear, is that of a singing bird," because the sound could actually be coming from a musical instrument or a loudspeaker.

Happiness

Online Etymology Dictionary: late 14c., "lucky, favored by fortune, being in advantageous circumstances, prosperous;" of events, "turning out well," from hap (n.) "chance, fortune" + -y. Sense of "very glad" first recorded late 14c. Meaning "greatly pleased and content" is from 1520s.

Happiness has the same root as *happen*, i.e. event, how something happens, turns out. Nothing else. The sense that happiness is only experienced if the outcome is good, is rather new (late 14th century). The sense "pleasant and contented mental state" is from the 1590s.

Happiness is originally completely independent of the opinions about an outcome. And it points very well to our true and fundamental nature: We are the happiness in which everything takes place, completely independent of how the outcome is perceived or assessed.

One definition of happiness that I feel matches this very well is *the absence of lack.*

Illusion

A false perception of reality due to ambiguous sense impressions. Note that an illusion is not the same as a lie. A lie does not have an underlying reality (e.g. a round two-dimensional square), but an illusion does (but it may not necessarily be the one I believe). Examples: A snake charmer's "snake" is an illusion, and its reality is the rope. A mirage is an illusion, and its reality is light.

The word **myth** (from the Greek *mýthos* = story, saga) is often confused with **lie**. A myth is a story where the details of it are not necessarily true, but the intent of the myth is that the message, the moral of the story, is true. Example: Santa Claus sees the thoughts and deeds of all children throughout the year and rewards them with Christmas gifts – or not – depending on how the child has behaved, is a myth, but the message that "good deeds are rewarded" is there (regardless if one agrees with that message or not).

Materialism

Wikipedia: "holds that matter is the fundamental substance in nature, and that all things, including mental states and consciousness, are results of material interactions of material things". It is closely related to *physicalism*. Its world view of reality starts with matter that gives rise to brains that give rise to minds that give rise to consciousness. The opposite to materialism is *idealism*, and its world view starts with consciousness, in which minds appear, in which the body and the world appears. See *Dualism*.

Meditation

From the Latin *meditari*, which means to think on, ponder, contemplate. The Tibetan word is *gom*, which means become familiar with, used to. To become familiar with our fundamental nature, which is something we can always contemplate, and it is actually not an activity, but simply being what is: Consciousness.

Metaphor

Wikipedia: "a figure of speech that, for rhetorical effect, directly refers to one thing by mentioning another." – often with the intent to point to something more complicated, in a simpler way.

Mind

Wikipedia: "that which thinks, imagines, remembers, wills, and senses, or is the set of faculties responsible for such phenomena." A mind is the localized activity of primary Consciousness, just like a whirlpool is the localized activity of the river.

Mystery

The word comes from the Indo-European *mu-*, that originally referred to certain movements of the lips, producing sound with closed lips, as in "to mutter".

The biggest mystery is impossible to speak, i.e. how something appears in and of time- and spaceless Consciousness. It is unmistakably known and experienced, but as soon as we try to speak of it (after the mind formulates thoughts about it, and the mouth tries to say it), it becomes a muttering with closed lips, because all thoughts and words are forms in that which they are trying to describe, and a form can never describe what it comes from, in the same way that a whirlpool in a river can never contain or encompass the river that it consists of.

Mystic

Summarizing various definitions found on the internet: A religious or philosophical view (mysticism), where the adherents (mystics) seek union with the etherial or divine, or experiential knowledge about the true reality by contemplatively immersing themselves in the inner experience.

Non-dualism

Wikipedia: "Reality does not consist of discrete, separate objects, but forms a unified whole which can be experienced as such". Unlike materialistic dualism, it expresses that reality consists of one and the same fundamental kind, property, nature, or essence. The word in Sanskrit is *advaita*, which means "not two," and it points to that reality does not consist of two natures that are separate from and independent of each other, e.g. observer/observed, matter/spirit, subject/object, etc. See *Dualism*.

Ontology

Wikipedia: "the philosophical study of being, as well as related concepts such as existence, becoming, and reality." From the Greek *ontos* + *logia* = the knowledge of being.

Order of magnitude

Wikipedia: "a level in a system used for measuring something in which each level is N times larger than the one before." I do not use this in a mathematical way in this book, rather it is a convenient expression to describe the order of the magnitudes of e.g. the microcosm, human, planet, galaxy, universe, consciousness, etc.

Perception

Wikipedia: "the organization, identification, and interpretation of sensory information in order to represent and understand the presented information or environment".

After sensations and sensing, perception happens. But perception is also of non-sensory things, e.g. thoughts and emotions. The word is from the Latin *perceptio* which means to take, gather, in the sense that data is collected in order to make an assessment about what has been experienced. The interpretation may or may not be accurate.

Person

 a part in a drama, assumed character, originally "a mask, a false face," such as those of wood or clay, covering the whole head, worn by the actors in later Roman theater.

What was originally expressed with this word has very little to do with how the word is used today. When the Latin word was first used, the meaning had nothing to do with what or who we are, our real nature, but rather with that of a mask being used by actors, and that how in life, we have different masks or roles, and that the mask is not what we truly are.

Philosophy

From the Greek *filos* + *sophia* = love of wisdom. Philosophy in modern academia is not what the word points to, which is the love of wisdom – not the knowledge of what constitutes philosophy or which philosophers said or meant what.

Real(ity)

In this book, it refers to that which in the direct experience is true and therefore real. The experiencing of a thought, dream, sound, or sight, are true and real (even though the content of a thought or dream, or the interpretation of a sound or sight may not be true). The common denominator is that something happens, appears, is done – out of, or in something. In our direct experience, it is always clear, real, and true, that everything happens, appears, and is done in and out of Consciousness.

Responsibility

Responsibility is often confused with *liability*.

Originally, *responsibility* had nothing to do with morals or law, but *liability* does. Responsibility is fundamentally the capacity or ability to respond to something. It came to be used for when someone was liable to be held accountable in legal matters, and it may be herein the confusion occurred.

Century Dictionary:
With regard to the legal use of the word, two conceptions are often confused — namely, that of the potential condition of being bound to answer or respond in case a wrong **should occur**, and that of the actual condition of being bound to respond because a wrong **has occurred**. For the first of these *responsible* is properly used, and for the second *liable*.

Informally, the capacity to respond is something we recognize: If someone calls me an idiot, I have the capacity to respond – but I'd rather not. Nor am I liable to do so.

Sense

Wikipedia: "a biological system used by an organism for sensation, the process of gathering information about the world through the detection of stimuli."

Solipsism

Wikipedia: "the philosophical idea that only one's mind is sure to exist"

Synchronicity

Wikipedia: "one's subjective experience that coincidences between events in one's mind and the outside world may be causally unrelated to each other yet have some other unknown connection."

True

Probably from Sanskrit *sat* = being, good, true, from the root *es* = to be. True is therefore related to "being," to be, and "is". If something **is**, it is true. The Bhagavad Gita says:

> *That which is, never ceases to be;*
> *that which is not, never comes into existence.*

I often write "what **Is**" and "that which **Is**," often with a capital letter, precisely in the sense that what **Is**, is True.